The McConnie Family of St. Vincent

(The Samuel Boxill McConnie family)

Published by Impact Publishing®, Lake Mary, FL.

Impact Publishing® is a registered trademark.

Printed in the United States of America.

ISBN: 979-8-9918645-1-0
LCCN: 2024926947

This publication is designed to provide accurate and authoritative information with regard to the subject matter covered. It is sold with the understanding that the publisher is not engaged in rendering legal, accounting, or other professional advice. If legal advice or other expert assistance is required, the services of a competent professional should be sought. The opinions expressed by the authors in this book are not endorsed by Impact Publishing® and are the sole responsibility of the author rendering the opinion.

Most Impact Publishing® titles are available at special quantity discounts for bulk purchases for sales promotions, premiums, fundraising, and educational use. Special versions or book excerpts can also be created to fit specific needs.

For more information, please write:
Impact Publishing®
P.O. Box 950370
Lake Mary, FL 32795
Tel: 1.877.261.4930

The McConnie Family of St.Vincent

(The Samuel Boxill McConnie family)

HISTORY & GENEALOGY OF A HUNDRED-YEAR FAMILY AFFAIR

(1870 to 1970)

Geoffrey B Nanton
(son of Ada Elaine Nanton née McConnie)

Impact Publishing®
Lake Mary, Florida

The Island of Saint Vincent

(Note: See Appendix C)

CONTENTS

McCONNIE FAMILY PICTURE

The Richard Alleyne & Mary Elizabeth Anne (Layne) McConnie Family
~ circa 1909 (likely taken at the family home in Ratho Mill, St. Vincent)

L to R: (i) Cecily Ermine (Cill), (ii) Dora Alinda (Lynn)-sitting,
(iii) Mary Olive Louise (Maisie), (iv) Richard Alleyne-sitting,
(v) Richard Cleve (Cleve)-standing, (vi) Ada Elaine (Ada) - youngest,
(vii) Mary Elizabeth Anne (Liz)–sitting, (viii) Julian O'Cara (Julian),
(ix) Betha Idalie (Betha)–sitting, (x) Stella Lavinia (Stella)

PREFACE

It will be useful for readers to note why this genealogical exercise was undertaken. I grew up interested in family relationships where family friends and acquaintances were often called Uncle and Aunt, regardless of our having no biological relationship. This was confusing at first, but as children, we soon accepted this cultural nuance as a part of the landscape. In addition, growing up in the fifties and sixties (1950s & 1960s) in St. Vincent gave me shades of a (Victorian/Edwardian) British colonial cultural upbringing that I now use to pass along my genealogical deductions and observations. These were days in St. Vincent when small children were to be seen and not heard, and the kindergarten tale of the birds and the bees was the cover story for discussions on where babies came from. Growing up, like all young teenagers, we soon found different and more confusing information on this subject from school mates and friends, and we were left to weed out truths as we matured.

My interest in genealogy burgeoned when I learned that E.R. (Ted) McConney of Portland, OR who had corresponded with my mother, Ada (McConnie) Nanton, had amassed information on a huge McConney family tree – his children referred to it as a family forest – genealogy that began in Barbados and spread throughout the world. In addition to his documented family tree recorded on a large sheet of paper about 3ft by 5ft – which I subsequently inherited from my mother – he compiled the genealogy of the McConneys. This was updated by his son, Gerry McConney, and subsequently further enhanced by my brother-in-law, Gerry Bowen (whose mother, Thelma Wood, was a McConnie descendent).

Ted McConney went on to become a member of the Barbados Museum and Historical Society and was recognized by the society for his work on the McConney family roots and their early settlement in Barbados dating back to the eighteenth century. He stated that the name "McConney" was likely a version of the Mcconahay or Mcconnahee surname found in the census and parish records in Barbados in the 1700s. These original names likely derive from a Gaelic form of the name. As far as was researched by Ted McConney, these McConneys were of Scottish origin, and would probably have arrived in Barbados as captured prisoners of war, exiled political enemies, indentured laborers or hardy sailors.

The McConnie history and details given here of the family in St. Vincent are principally that of Samuel Boxill McConnie's first family. A short genealogy is included on his second family, but there is no coverage of other McConneys who may have moved to St. Vincent at the same time. While it is certainly possible that there were others with the same family name involved in their historic migration in 1875, the author cannot speak to their possible experiences, as he has found no additional information or record of them. And so, for the purposes of this study, it is assumed that the McConnie families discussed here were the only McConnies involved in the migration to St. Vincent.

I have collected a significant amount of additional information on both the McConnie and Nanton families over the years. This collection was made possible through family, friends, government records, church records and the internet. Many records are readily available on the internet – especially for Barbados – which I would encourage all amateur genealogists to utilize. St. Vincent and the Grenadines do have some available genealogy information on the internet, but it is not extensive. My research extended to wills, land deed records and legal documents that I was able to find. The result is a blend of genealogy and history of a slice of Vincentian life from 1870 to 1970.

I particularly wish to mention my mother's role as an accurate and reliable source. Ada Elaine (McConnie) Nanton was an assiduous and precise gatherer of facts and records of her family, even prior to her meeting Ted McConney and subsequently when spurred on by his research efforts. In addition, I wish to document the unfathomable change in the family-name spelling from McConney to McConnie. From all accounts and records, this altered spelling was a corruption of the name McConney, with no explanation given, and occurred only in the Vincentian McConney/McConnie family name.

Some of the families migrating from Barbados to St. Vincent in 1875 would have had trade and laboring experiences that they could rely on to help them financially. Many would probably have been involved in some kind of agriculture. Either way, they all would likely have had kitchen gardens around their homes to help feed themselves. This produce could also have been used for trade or barter. Because of the significance of the agriculturally-based economy in St. Vincent, I have also included some brief geographical input of the island.

In the introduction that follows, I will offer some brief notes on the history, geography, and sociology of the island – which may help those in the family who have never visited St. Vincent – to understand how these factors affected the lives of the McConnie Clan in particular. In Appendix A that follows the family information, I give some detail on the modernization of the island. Also, if any of my personal input is offensive to some readers, please remember that it was intended to help flesh out living conditions in the day and age of the period in which they lived. This study was not intended to be offensive, but in the documentation of my personal interpretation of the era of the Vincentian McConnies, it will inevitably contain some unintended inaccuracies, errors and omissions.

Finally, please note that I have tried to use only documented dates or dates from trusted sources. As all genealogists are aware, dates given on hand-written government and church records are generally accurate, but, as in the case of all hand-written records, they should always be regarded with a hint of suspicion unless corroborated. These errors could be clerical, a result of misinformation given for the event (pronounced, written or spelled inaccurately by the information supplier), or because of the time-consuming nature of researching and recording essentially boring government records and statistical data by myself.

N.B. If you should find erroneous/missing information in this submission, please do not hesitate to contact the author with substantiated corrections so that he can update it for potential future editions, if any. (Email: thenantons@aol.com)

-------<<<<<oOo>>>>>-------

ACKNOWLEDGMENTS

It would be difficult to list everyone who supplied information, encouragement and support, but, without their input, this book history and genealogy could not have been compiled. So, to each and every one of those un-named people who assisted, I wish to take this opportunity to thank you for your invaluable help.

However, I would be remiss if I do not thank the following individuals by name – First of all, to my immediate family – Ada (McConnie) Nanton, Mac Nanton and Jen Sauter. Next, a huge shout-out to my cousin Philip Nanton who read my drafts and kept me and my contents on track, to Connor DeMerchant who supplied key data through his boots-on-the ground research in St. Vincent, Barbados and the UK, and to cousins Randy Johnson and his sister, Iris Salcedo, who supplied photos and detailed information of the Puerto Rican side of the family.

Then, my deep gratitude to my book designer and good friend, Ted Gonzalez, who was especially helpful in managing my multiple draft permutations, combinations and revisions. Adding to Ted's invaluable help, my niece Alison Sauter was instrumental in designing and enhancing the cover graphically.

Finally, without the patience and forbearance of my wife, Helen, as well as the understanding of Andy and Nick and their families, none of this would have been possible. Helen was especially supportive of my determination to get this information into print for succeeding generations and, as she referred to it, my passion for 'digging up bones'.

Now, I would be remiss not to mention our grands, the joy of our lives – in order of seniority: Brock, Bowen, Oliver, Addie and Celeste. They were the catalyst that propelled me to complete this book.

INTRODUCTION

A Condensed History, Geography, and Sociology of the Era under Review (1870-1970) In St. Vincent and the Grenadines

St. Vincent is a small (150 sq. mile) island country in the Caribbean Sea. This island is the aftermath of volcanic upheaval over past eons and is a part of the volcanic island chain in the Caribbean known as the Windward and Leeward islands. In addition to the Windward and Leeward Islands, the islands of Barbados, the Bahamas, Trinidad & Tobago, and Jamaica all formed part of a geographic grouping known for centuries as the British West Indies, most of which are now independent. St. Vincent, following the lead of many of the former British colonies in the Caribbean, achieved independent nation status in 1979. The country of St. Vincent also encompasses a number of smaller islands known as the Grenadines (including Bequia, Union Island, Mustique, Mayreau, Canouan, and Palm Island). The Grenadines are currently known internationally as a yachter's haven. Geo-politically, St. Vincent is currently referred to as St. Vincent and the Grenadines (SVG).

Because of its mountainous topography, St. Vincent was a difficult island for Europeans to settle and develop economically four hundred years ago. Its mountainous terrain made it forbidding and somewhat of a fortress – a factor used to their advantage by the native Caribs and Arawaks, and subsequently by invading French and British forces from the seventeenth through the twentieth centuries. For the most part, Spain, a leading world power in the fifteenth and sixteenth centuries, was too busy trying to find El Dorado/gold in South America, colonizing larger islands (e.g., Puerto Rico and Cuba), and conducting the Spanish Inquisition, to get involved in battles for small Caribbean islands. Colloquially speaking, Spain was "The Big Cheese!" in international terms at that time.

St. Vincent's mountainous upside is that it is a bountiful haven for agriculture due to its fertile volcanic soil, but its major downside is that mechanical or large-scale farming is very difficult. From a strategic point of view, the mountainous geography of the island would have aided and abetted military leaders especially in the eighteenth and nineteenth centuries, but the topography really impeded all previous periods of settlement and domination, whether native or foreign, in defending this island from outside attack.

Historically, this island passed through the control of indigenous Amerindians and Caribs, followed by the French and the English. The Treaty of Paris in 1783, a major international treaty, was the treaty in which France ceded a portion of North America along with several small Caribbean islands, including St. Vincent, to the English Government. It became an outpost in the British Empire.

Like all islands in the West Indies, St. Vincent was involved in the slave trade in the 18th and 19th centuries, and today, its population is mainly of African descent (approx. 98%), with a small number of mixed-race descendants. By and large, current Vincentian society is a melting pot of African, Carib, Anglo, East Indian, Middle Eastern, Portuguese, and Asian descendants. Because of this mix, it will be useful to address the racial underlay in this genealogy. It would be unrealistic to present the McConney saga that follows without recognition of the racial relations that existed in the period under discussion and which would have affected their economic survival and social mobility.

The Vincentian Black slave population was emancipated in the first half of the nineteenth century. We clearly understand that from all accounts of that period, emancipation was not a propulsion from dependence to prosperity, it was merely a start. I do not know the local history of the early period intimately, but it is not a stretch to think that it would take generations for the freed Black population to be absorbed into Vincentian working society – one that was notably divided into the haves and have-nots mainly by skin-color in the nineteenth century.

At the time of the 1875 McConney migration, Vincentian society was still trying to assimilate the freed Black population (emancipation was in 1834) into its economy. Many Black people, especially those in more remote areas, were ekeing out a living, and had a difficult time finding gainful employment to meet their most basic needs. It is probable that many relied on handouts and bartered labor for food. To make economic progress, it would take many years for the Black population to establish itself securely.

St. Vincent was never a prosperous colony, and to my knowledge, the ruling colonial elite of the era under discussion (late 1800s to mid-1900s) – which consisted of British Administration expatriates and the plantocracy – did not have any significant interest in improving economic conditions for locals. Then, if you add the class division of nineteenth-century English culture into the equation, there was no special interest or compelling reason to elevate Black people, mixed race or lower class White people economically. The result was that social and economic changes would undergo a long and painful transition that lasted well into the twentieth century.

As the McConnies were digging themselves out of poverty where they settled in Glen, the twentieth century brought many racial challenges to St. Vincent. These culminated in the race riots of 1935 in St. Vincent that were aimed at the British Colonial Govt. Administration. The Black population protested their poor social, health and financial conditions as compared with the White population. From what I gathered from family members, the McConnies were probably insulated from serious racial backlash from these riots in St. Vincent, because they were neither a large and powerful group nor were they politically-active antagonists.

The McConnies also tended to live closely within the 'Redleg' community bubble for survival. The 'Redleg' label was originally applied to 'poor white' Barbadian field hands. They were called 'redlegs' – so named because their fair skins would turn red, sunburn and blister in the hot tropical sun, presenting a huge problem for European laborers working in the fields in a tropical agricultural economy.

The education of the Vincentian population – starting in the early 1900s – was, probably, single-handedly one of the most important factors that helped to improve living conditions of the Black population. While education in and of itself is not a panacea for all racial issues, as was evidenced in the 1935 race riots, it contributed a substantial improvement for the prospects of the Black community. They were able to develop a louder and more 'visible' voice in the 1940s, which led to the rise of trade unionism (Prime Minister E.T. Joshua comes to mind) which had both economic and political clout.

By 1951, the island officially approved universal adult suffrage – which allowed island-wide representation and leadership for the Black population in Government. By the time I left St. Vincent for Canada in 1966, there was a small and growing, but firmly-established, educated Black professional and business middle and upper class in the community, which added a substantial degree of stability to Vincentian society. This would ensure the continuing progress of Vincentians of colour in the future.

The 'Redlegs' in St. Vincent, people like the McConnies, were undoubtedly helped by a measure of 'white privilege', as innocent as that may have seemed at the time. However, after universal adult suffrage (1951) was government-mandated, democratic voting ensured a Black counterbalance of leadership and power on the island. Initially, racial relations deteriorated, scaring the small white population. This relationship ebbed and flowed over the coming years, morphing into an era where democratic rule prevailed and Black leadership was firmly established. By the

1960s, although there were pockets of racial intolerance, there was never outright racial warfare. The Vincentian attitude to race, with only a few exceptions, could be attributed to parents of every background, who encouraged their children to treat everyone, regardless of race, creed, or color, with respect. My immediate family mixed freely and enjoyed social mobility in the island as did many others. In fact, the society was, even then, a blended mix.

As a whole, by the 1960s, the Vincentian population had largely developed some measure of mutual respect and peaceful existence between races. Not surprisingly, it still harbored elements of discontent. Extreme fringe elements on both sides of racial relations (notably, but not exclusively, the extremes of the wealthy and the poor) often were willing to stir up animosity within their own circles. However, on balance, this adversity continued to prod both sides to adopt more rational ways to live together for mutual advancement. There were still many inequities (especially noticeable in property and business ownership, as well as in the small percentage of Black professionals), but racial differentiation was shifting, and it was replaced by more of a class-type system of discrimination. It should be noted that the shift in power to the Black population in the 1950s kept race relations in St. Vincent from sliding back into the abyss of resentment, repression, and civil unrest prevalent between the races during the previous hundred years, but it was not erased easily – that would take much longer.

When the islanders looked for opportunities for personal improvement, regardless of skin color, one answer that never changed for Vincentians was that of migration. Vincentians of every creed, color and background migrated—mostly to the United Kingdom, the USA and to Canada. While aspiring to better jobs and a better standard of living, many also left the island in order to pursue higher education. Unfortunately for St. Vincent, only a few returned. This had the classic 'brain-drain' effect on the island. Migration offered an opportunity to get ahead financially far more rapidly than the local economy could offer, and as a result, it never stopped. This 'brain drain' in St. Vincent (as in all West Indian islands) would persist throughout the twentieth century and beyond.

As regards world unrest in the 100-year period under review, St. Vincent in general, and the McConnie family in particular, were not seriously affected by outside world conflicts. The factors of (1) small-island geographic isolation, (2) an insular view of the world, and (3) home pressures to survive in a poor, undeveloped economy – all insulated and shielded the Vincentian population from external conflicts (such as the Spanish-American War of 1898 and World Wars I & II among many others). There was merely a handful of conscripts from St. Vincent who entered the aforementioned wars during the period under review. However, to my knowledge, aside from imported foods, oils, synthetics and other miscellaneous import shortages, there was no recorded significant effect on the vast majority of Vincentians at home.

The island of St. Vincent was never the most sought-after colonial jewel in the Antilles for Great Britain in the years under review. While the original settlers, the Arawaks and the Caribs, as well as the Europeans and Africans that followed, enjoyed the fruits of the soil and the sea as residents, St. Vincent was never an easy place to establish settlements, commerce, or international trade. Its topography, up to the present, primarily accommodates agriculture and eco-tourism with a smattering of manufacturing, and severely limits the ease of transportation and large-scale agriculture. This has been a challenge to its political and economic progress and has made it difficult to provide its population a higher standard of living over the years.

However, a previously underdeveloped part of the island archipelago, the Grenadines, has contributed significantly to the economic wellbeing of St. Vincent in the tourist sector. And perhaps there may be other unknown and untapped natural resources waiting to be discovered. Also, while the volcano, La Soufriere, has been a dubious tourist attraction, it has been both a spectacle and a source of local and international concern when it erupted violently in 1718, 1812, 1902, 1979, and most recently in 2021.

In spite of difficult topographic, economic and social conditions, the population of St. Vincent in the 100-year timeframe 1870 to 1970 – including the McConnie migrants – survived and made significant progress on this small island.

----<<<<oOo>>>>----

CHAPTER 1

THE McCONNIE MIGRATION

The McConnie migration from Barbados to St. Vincent in the nineteenth century began when a number of Barbadians (known as redlegs/'poor whites') were recruited by a Parish Rector in St. Joseph, Barbados. The move to St. Vincent started in 1861 by a Bradshaw family. Others moved in succeeding years, followed by the McConneys around 1875 (the only documented date I could find). The migration move from Barbados to St. Vincent spanned a distance of about 90 miles as the crow flies across the Caribbean Sea. At that time, the Barbados economy was in tatters as the world price of sugar – its main export – had plummeted due to over-production and over-supply from South America (Brazil) and East India, as well as the two Caribbean islands of Cuba and Jamaica.

The resulting high level of unemployment at that time (in the 19th century), as well as the dense population of Barbados, pushed the British-administered government and the plantocracy, both local and absentee, to encourage any migration in order to avoid civil and economic unrest on the island. The reduction of the agriculturally-dependent labor force in Barbados that depended on sugar cane production for their livelihood was particularly important to both the Barbados economy and the standard of living of laboring Barbadians (aka Bajans). In the mid-1850s, poor Barbadians of every stripe were barely eking out a living as there was a dearth of work for compensation, and living conditions were growing steadily worse.

The population of Barbados in the last half of the nineteenth century consisted of the ruling British Administration, the plantocracy, a small professional class of land managers, a few business traders, freed slaves and their descendants,[1] as well as working class and 'poor whites'. (The total population would have included mixed race descendants in all groups.) The Black population was considered hardier and better suited to working in the sugar cane fields than Whites by the plantocracy. Consequently, Whites were not desirable laborers; therefore, there was less incentive for the government or the plantocracy to try to keep them on the island. This 'perfect storm' for the economy of Barbados occurred in the first half of the 19th century and precipitated the migration of 'poor white' Barbadians as is detailed below. This was the 19th century era when 'Britannia (still) Ruled the Waves.'

And so it was, by the 1860s, that the opportunity arose for some 'redlegs' in the north-eastern area in Barbados (known as the Scotland district) to migrate to St. Vincent. The migration to St. Vincent in the period 1861 to 1875 consisted of an estimated 300 to 400 people who voluntarily made the move. To my knowledge, no official record, or unofficial record for that matter, even exists of the number or names of all those that migrated. In addition, a smaller number of the 'poor whites' migrated to Grenada (Mt. Moritz) around the same time, and a few more moved to small neighboring islands (like Bequia) in this migratory wave.

Interestingly, the larger islands (Jamaica and Trinidad) did not want any immigrants from this group as they saw them only as a financial and civic burden. However, their move to the islands of St. Vincent and Grenada, both of which were willing to accept

---

1. The Atlantic slave trade was ended by Britain in the period 1807-1833 and in America in 1863, and the black population was about 85% of the total population in Barbados.

them, suggests these islands were able to accommodate them and needed them for the further development of their lands. Additionally, the volcanic soils in both St. Vincent and Grenada were especially fertile. In fact, there is an old Vincentian saying which states, "our volcanic soil is so fertile (and constantly bathed by rain) that if you stick your finger in the ground, it will grow."

Most of the migrating 'poor white' Barbadians who went to St. Vincent settled in an area called Dorsetshire Hill where they settled down on local estate lands. They would have traveled to St. Vincent in small groups, as the ships of the day (mostly schooners and a few larger sailing ships plying the islands), could not have taken large numbers of passengers as well as their baggage, livestock and belongings.

Among the Barbadian 'redleg' migrants of that period, the McConney, Gill, and Layne families were among the last families who migrated, and they settled in the Glen/Ratho Mill area near the town of Calliaqua. This area was some three miles distant 'up-hill-and-down-dale' from Dorsetshire Hill as the crow flies. Dorsetshire Hill was also a former hillside military stronghold (used strategically at different times by the Caribs, the French and the British).

The McConney/Layne/Gill group of families who settled in the Calliaqua/Ratho Mill area known as Glen, were allowed to do so by nearby plantation owners. It is interesting to note that many in this group of families, and possibly other settlers, brought with them trades backgrounds in addition to a knowledge of planting and livestock farming for survival. The trades included shopkeepers, shoemakers, blacksmiths and seamstresses (as noted on official records from both Barbados and St. Vincent).

Whatever the case, one assumption is that the land there may have been easier to access and cultivate, being somewhat less mountainous than other unused and uncultivated lands such as at Dorsetshire Hill. Being not as mountainous, perhaps it was easier to get land in the Ratho Mill area into agricultural production faster. A major reason for settling these families in this area, is that the owners of those lands up behind Calliaqua needed land tenants and cheap labor. They would have been a ready supply of cheap migrant labor for land-owners estates (Ratho Mill, Brighton, etc.) in that area.

It was previously mentioned that the McConney group and the Dorsetshire Hill 'poor white' settlers from Barbados had a history of being largely of Scottish origin. The McConney group seemed to have kept this traditional background. I recall hearing my mother singing and hummimg old Scottish/British songs she had learned as a girl. On the whole, the Barbadian 'poor white' migrants in St. Vincent tended to be clannish, and they kept up their Scottish/English heritage and customs as passed down to them.

Language used in the island is English, with an occasional word of French derivation – due to prior French occupation (e.g., 'tantie' - from the French 'tante' for aunt). The general language St. Vincent used was English, but Vincentians of every stripe are renowned for an accent that deletes the last syllable from words, pronounces the 'th' sound as a 't', and using the broad 'a' in their everyday speech. In the period under review, there were a number of St. Vincent-based English administrative officials that were there to oversee government adherence and conformity to the Mother Country's policies. These expatriates would have played a role in establishing the use of English in all schools. Needless to mention, some Vincentians tried to elevate their social status by adopting an English accent, but they were usually perceived as oddities.

Ratho Mill was, at the time, regarded as a rural area. My mother, Ada Elaine McConnie, who was born there, always referred to the area as Glen. I hope to find documentation some day indicating why they settled here. At this point, however, it is likely they entered St. Vincent via the Kingstown harbour, as there is no proof to the contrary. This being the case, their relocation to Glen in Calliaqua would have been an involved logistical move.

CHAPTER 2

SERVICES & INFRASTRUCTURE PERSPECTIVE ON ST. VINCENT – 1870 TO 1970

Education

Per my mother, Ada Nanton (née McConnie), the McConnies had a very high regard for education. I touch on this subject as an integral part of their upbringing. From my father, I understand that both of her brothers, Richard Cleve and Julian, attended the St. Vincent Agricultural School. When the McConneys moved to St. Vincent, education was of major importance to them, but obviously, education could not trump surviving in a new country and new environment, especially with the daunting task of making a living and a better future for themselves and families.

I do recall my mother stating that her mother went to school in Barbados and enjoyed a brief period of education there. I know that Mama, Mary Elizabeth Anne McConnie, as well as Papa, Richard Alleyne McConnie, were literate, and that they passed their basic skills on to their children. I also note that their two sons, Richard Cleve and Julian, along with their two youngest daughters, Aunt Maisie (Mary Olive Louise) and my mother (Ada

31

Elaine), were their only children who attended (public) secondary schools in St. Vincent. Ada noted in her written records that she went to the Girls High School at age 16 in 1922 for 2 or 3 years. She had a solid grounding in English Literature and Language, Mathematics, History and French, all of which she passed for her Junior School Certificate.[2]

I think it is reasonable to assume that all the McConnie children in this family had early basic schooling in "the three Rs" at home. I believe that the four eldest girls – Alinda, Betha, Cecily and Stella – had little if any formal education, but they were, nonetheless, literate, having been schooled at home.

It is noteworthy that Richard Alleyne's eldest son, Cleve (Richard Cleve) was able to use his agricultural education from the St. Vincent Agricultural School to go on to manage sugar cane plantations in Puerto Rico, and also became a sugar scientist there for the Fajardo Sugar Company. While his brother Julian never followed in Cleve's sugar-research footsteps, the promotions he received on the job in Puerto Rico suggest he was a competent agriculturalist as well as a good manager. Julian had a brief stint working in Cuba, but was uncomfortable with the political unrest (during the Fulgencia Batista era) and returned to Puerto Rico. He lived the rest of his life in Puerto Rico.

Transportation

When my mother told me how proud her father was to be able to buy a horse when he lived at Ratho Mill (late 1800s) – for personal use as well as to transport agricultural produce to town – it seemed to me that her comment was a suggestion that he had moved up financially. Bear in mind that the distance to ride or walk to town (Kingstown, the capital) from Ratho Mill was

---

2. The Junior School Certificate was an overseas certification used in the British system. You would have to wait months for the exam results to be sent by 'surface mail' to and from England for grading before you knew whether you passed or failed.

about six miles. While this was not an impossibly long distance for walking, in addition to the very hilly and often muddy and slippery terrain, treks to town would have to be coordinated with the weather. (The average annual rainfall in St. Vincent is approximately 95 inches/year.) As a boy, it seemed to me that it rained every day.

I do not have any specific record of the McConnie use of bicycles, but I suspect that Richard Alleyne McConnie owned and used one for daily travel to work from Richmond Hill/Frenches to Kingstown in the 1920s and 1930s. It is probable that his sons would have used bicycles as well, but their sisters probably did not. I know my mother could ride a bike, but she never owned one to my knowledge. I was born when she was 41 years old.

Another milestone for the McConnies was when my mother, Ada Elaine, purchased a motor car in the 1930s. She was a government clerk and while living at home, saved the means to buy a car before she got married. She told me on more than one occasion, she called on different men (including Dad before they were married) to crank the motor to start her car – there were no electric starters in those days. She also got Dad or a cousin to repair it for her as required. She told me that she was the first woman to buy and drive their own car in St. Vincent.

Health

The Vincentian population seemed reasonably healthy during the period in question, but having no medical background, I leave a health analysis to those better informed. I do recall that up to the 1950s and 60s, malnutrition was a major problem, especially in infants. Infant mortality was high and one of the highest in the British colonies. Growing up in the 1950s and 1960s, fevers and respiratory diseases typical of a tropical environment were rampant.

Like the general population, the McConnies tended to self-medicate in the absence of qualified medical help. Most

Vincentians would take their medication advice from a pharmacist. He would diagnose and then prescribe whatever medication in his stock that could help. There were no medicines on a do-not-take list – whether antibiotics, morphine or any other drugs. All available remedies and drugs were used. While many in the younger Vincentian population seemed reasonably healthy to me during the period in question, there were many issues with medical care availability that told a sad tale of inadequate health care.

I left St. Vincent in mid-1966, so I cannot make any personal health observations on the general health of the Vincentian population beyond that time, but maintaining good health was always a concern when I was growing up. As in all underdeveloped countries, self-medication and home remedies were often the only available health-help available. There were a variety of bush teas, laxatives and methods used to maintain good health or cure ill health – or so our parents thought. Worming for children was considered routine and administered by family members or friends as part of everyday life. The unscientific concept of "if-it-tastes-bad-it-must-be-good-for-you" was a normal part of Vincentian life and culture.

I also recall my grandmother (on the Nanton side – Granny Nanton) kept a jar of leeches (yuch! they were not a pretty sight) to bleed off 'bad blood' that affected the body. My brother told me that he was the recipient of one of those sessions for his catarrh as a boy. I personally took a variety of awful-tasting bush teas and laxatives to rid my body of whatever impurity I was supposed to have. These included senna, Epsom salts, fish oils and cod liver oil. As a boy, these remedies seemed far worse than any health problems they were supposed to alleviate, but they were administered none the less.

Nutrition and Food

All McConnies I knew loved their food. Throughout their residence in St. Vincent up into the 1960s, they grew and raised much of their own food. The families kept chickens and grew numerous fruits, vegetables, and beans. The McConnies would have enjoyed a diet of fish, breadfruit, ground provisions and fruit, with some chicken, lamb or shellfish thrown in occasionally. Beef was more expensive and local beef that could be purchased in St. Vincent often was harvested from milk cows and bulls that had seen far too many birthdays, and their meat was first cousin to shoe leather.

Nutrition is always the product of availability and cost of food. St. Vincent had a ready supply of fish, ground provisions and fruit, most of which were homegrown, cheap and plentiful. Livestock meats available locally were limited and not very cheap by comparison. Imports were more expensive, and the merchants/ wholesalers in Kingstown made money by importing cheap supplements—(Irish) potatoes, rice from Guyana, and salted codfish from Newfoundland. Consequently, feeding most of the population was accomplished by using locally-grown fruit and vegetables, fish, and livestock, along with imported foodstuffs for those who could afford it.

Animals raised domestically for meat included chickens, sheep, goats, pigs, and cows. So, while there was some availability of chicken, lamb, goat, pork and beef, it tended to be expensive. (I clearly recall that local beef was tough, and the cow milk often tasted peculiar because of the contaminants ingested during their grazing.) As one can imagine, theft of livestock was common in a poor community (tracing the origin of meat after it was slaughtered was impossible). Some meats could only be classified as 'mystery meats.'

The Vincentian population also harvested small quantities of land crabs and crayfish, along with any other sources of sea food that they could obtain (viz., conchs, eels, turtles, whalemeat and octopus).

Early Lighting & Energy Sources

(Author's Note: The tropical daylight hours in St. Vincent are typically between 6 am and 6 pm – with some variations around the annual solstices – as St. Vincent lies close to the Equator.)

Finding efficient and inexpensive sources of energy to provide light at night was an important economic factor in the life of Vincentians. The use of candles and oil lamps in St. Vincent to provide light in the period under review was necessary and pervasive. Kerosene lamps and lanterns were frequently used at night and most dwellings had them. Kerosene was imported as were candles (made from a variety of animal and vegetable fats and oils). In St. Vincent, both oil lamps and candles were used until electrical light and power was available.

Kerosene oil was also used for powering both cooking stoves and refrigerators, both items of which the McConnies purchased in the 1950s. Cooking with charcoal or wood was also a reliable means of cooking, and these would have been used by most Vincentians – including the McConnies in Glen – up into the 1950s. The coals were burnt in a coal pot and wood was burnt under a metal grid or under pots or food suspended from above. For the McConnies and most Vincentians, used appliances were resold and repaired and went through many hands before being sent to garbage heaven. (Sadly, the sea probably got much of it.).

The capital of Kingstown had oil lamp light poles set up from about the 1920s, and before that, candle and lamp light from buildings was all that was available, unless it was a moonlight night. In fact, many students of the era under discussion studied by candle or lamp light because of an unreliable electrical supply.

As noted in the following sections on communications and electricity, some rural areas were still not being served by an electrical supply up to when I left St. Vincent in 1966.

Electricity

Electricity became available to homeowners in Kingstown sometime in the 1930s. The McConnies had their wooden house wired – probably in the late 1930s or early 1940s by a cousin, Dillon Gill. He had worked in New York on the electrical power grid in the 1920s. I recall the ceramic and Bakelite/phenolic fixtures used in the electrification of their house. The Bakelite material was a competent insulator, but it was brittle and fragile, so switches were replaced quite often.

Communications (Air & Surface Mail/Cable telegrams/ Telephones/Radio)

For communications, the early McConnies in St. Vincent would have had to rely on word-of-mouth, post cards, letters and notes to connect with each other locally and overseas. Locally, calling and shouting over distances between houses and across valleys probably worked to some degree. In those days, all mail was sent throughout the world by land and sea—surface mail. Air mail started in St. Vincent in 1927, and grew in fits and starts to a somewhat more regular service in the 1930s.

It was not until the 1930s that the St. Vincent Government Administration bought and installed a used wired-telephone system from the USA for St. Vincent. The telephone system I grew up with in the 1950s was of the old exchange-type vintage, where an attendant at the main exchange in Kingstown asked who you wished to contact and then they connected both parties with wired plugs. You remained on the line while they rang the phoneline of the party you wished to speak with. Of course, there were also the party lines that required one, two or three rings to call and speak to the right party. (My home phone number in the 1960s, for example, was a mere two digits – our number was 97. (Side note on mail: In the 1950s and 1960s, my family's P.O. Box number was 55 and there was never any house delivery of mail. All mail in the town was picked up at the Kingstown Post Office.)

A telegram (cable) service was also established for the islands sometime in the first half of the twentieth century – in the 1920s or 1930's? I do not know a date for this, but telegrams (cables) were used in the 1940s to send critical information in a timely manner, and by the 1950s, no wedding was complete without cable wishes being read at the reception from family or friends overseas. The telegram service was made possible by a wire cable that physically connected St. Vincent, as part of a chain network with other neighboring islands, to England and the U.S.A.

In the 1940s and 50s, a long distance telephone call overseas was commercially available to Vincentians through the UK company, Cable & Wireless, Ltd. Callers would have to book a call with the overseas operator of the country in question ahead of the calling date. They would then have to go to the Kingstown office of Cable & Wireless and hope atmospherics on that day would permit them to speak to their desired party. This was far from a perfect system and often seemed like a three-ring circus because of the number of variables involved at each end.

There was very limited communication by 'ham radio' in the 1960s and 70s, and possibly earlier, but it was used primarily in emergencies.

Old Family Photographs

I have unearthed very few story details in the life of Richard Alleyne and Mary Elizabeth Anne McConnie. Consequently, I have had to rely on stories handed down, official and personal records, and photos, to interpret their lifestyle. Thankfully, the photographs of the McConnie family that have been found and handed down show that they had posed and sombre family pictures taken. In those old photos, they were dressed in their Sunday-best that was typical of the late 1800s or early 1900s. They were well shod and appeared well groomed. The pictures show a rather staid and serious looking group.

Overview

From the accomplishments of their children, we know the McConnies were industrious, quiet, focused and hard-working, and lived their lives devoted to helping themselves and their children improve their lot in life. As a result of close family proximity and the necessity for working together efficiently and effectively, they built close family relationships. This did not mean that their relationships were always harmonious, and there was certainly an underlying competitiveness that could easily breed jealousy – common to all families. I also believe that the Barbadian migrant families in the small island environment in St. Vincent were earnest and determined competitors who gave no quarter in their quest to survive and thrive.

For the most part, I do not know if McConnie dysfunction ever reached the proverbial level of the Hatfields and the McCoys.[3] As far as I am aware, better judgement prevailed, and family relationships were usually supportive. However, it is very likely that the close living, keen competition and limited resources on the island would have initiated some level of conflict in the two Samuel Boxill McConnie families. However, my concept of life in that McConnie world is a purely personal opinion.

There was a story of the family's involvement in rebuilding the Anglican church in Calliaqua, the area in which they settled, but I cannot find any confirmation of this, so that remains hearsay for now. I was told they went to church religiously, and the Anglican religion was the religion in which succeeding generations for the period under discussion were raised.

---

3. The Hatfields and the McCoys were fictional feuding families in the mountains of Kentucky. They were made out to enjoy exchanging insults and firing shotguns at each other in a feud for supremacy in arguments.

Reader's Notes

CHAPTER 3

SAMUEL BOXILL McCONNIE
(1835-1908)

Our family grouping that moved to the Glen/Ratho Mill area was headed by Samuel Boxill McConney (1835-1908). Samuel Boxill McConnie was my great grandfather and changed the spelling of his name from **McConney** to **McConnie**. His migration to St. Vincent was completely voluntary, especially considering the living conditions in Barbados at that time which were covered earlier. The logistics for such a move must have been complicated. Both he and his wife Marianna, and his wife's sister, Georgina, and all their children, of which eleven were born in Barbados, would have taken along as many of their possessions (including livestock) as they were allowed to carry to their new country.

However meagre, the possessions they carried would need to be mentally and/or physically inventoried and transported – starting from their abodes in Barbados to the new locations in St. Vincent. We are told that the Rector of the Parish of St.Joseph in Barbados had spearheaded the move for these migrants to St. Vincent. Again, to my knowledge, no records of this move appear to exist anywhere, but it would have been logistically complex for the organizers of the hundreds who were transported.

Samuel Boxill McConnie was born in Barbados in 1835 and

died in 1908 in St. Vincent, at the age of 73. His wife, Marianna Phillips, was born in Barbados in 1841, (she was six years younger than Samuel), and died in 1923 in St. Vincent. At 23, Samuel married Marianna (who was 15 years old at the time) on Nov. 11th, 1858 in Barbados. Samuel was listed as a shoemaker on the marriage register of the Parish Church of St. Joseph, and a shopkeeper on his first son's birth registration. Marianna's name did not show any occupation at the time of their marriage. They had nine children, of whom six were born in Barbados, and the three youngest in St. Vincent, where they settled.

Marianna Phillips became Samuel's wife in Barbados in 1858. She had her first child, Richard Alleyne in 1860 at 19. On moving to St. Vincent around 1875, Samuel Boxill McConney changed the spelling of his family name from McConney to McConnie – for reasons unknown. I have been unable to find any reason why this name-spelling change was made. I queried it, but even my mother (Samuel's granddaughter) had no explanation for this. Conjecture might consider it a spelling error, a purposeful change (for reasons good or bad), or simply a case of indifference. In any event, this group was not likely concerned with the spelling accuracy of their name, as compared with their need to survive.

In addition to the ten children that Samuel Boxill McConnie fathered with his wife Marianna (nee Phillips), Samuel fathered a second family concurrently with his wife's sister, Georgina (Lyder) Phillips, (ca.1832–1917) who he never married. They produced about seven children. Samuel also brought this second family with him to St. Vincent from Barbados at the same time. His second family was raised under a different roof to his first family, and he also gave his children his surname, McConnie. His children with Georgina (as listed by Ted McConney) were Edward, Aletha Ann (died at 13 mos.), Frederick Bowen, Aletha Blanche, Martha, Janet, and Joseph Isaiah. There is some doubt as to whether Samuel was the father of two of the children of whom she is listed as the mother – Edward and Frederick Bowen McConnie. (Then there were sons Samuel Foster Christopher and Joseph Alexander Lyder with no father listed). Between both families, Samuel Boxill fathered at least fifteen children on record that we know about – a busy man.

How Samuel managed both families at the same time was never discussed in my presence, but it must have required extraordinary emotional, financial, and mental gymnastics for the two family groups to cope with this unusual relationship. Undoubtedly, it likely made for emotional discussions, not to mention great gossip in the community at large, and within the family in particular.

The names Georgina and Georgiana appear in the Barbados Parish Records interchangeably, but official records support the fact that they were likely one and the same person. Finally, the records researched cannot offer conclusive proof that Marianna and Georgina/Georgiana were sisters or half-sisters. Either way, this historical saga is not adversely affected. The major subject covered in this account is the family of Samuel Boxill and Marianna (nee Phillips) McConnie, and centers around their eldest son, Richard Alleyne McConnie, and his family. The remaining siblings in their first family are included in a condensed summary following genealogical and general information gathered on Richard Alleyne's children. The second family of Samuel Boxill McConnie and Georgina/Georgiana (Lyder) Phillips follows the more detailed information of Samuel's first family in a very limited manner. I hope family readers who can add more information on his second family will record more details of this family before the information is lost or forgotten.

I was never privy to any confidential information on the above family matter, and, in my generation, the family relationships were accepted for what they were, and they were tolerated by those involved. Suffice it to say that this McConnie family offspring in St. Vincent had a plethora of cousins and half cousins. Fortunately, as children, we mixed and played together without any expressed or indicated concern for this glorious, tangled and confused family relationship.

CHAPTER 4

SAMUEL BOXILL McCONNIE'S FIRST FAMILY

Samuel Boxill and Marianna's children were:

1. Richard Alleyne McConnie (1860-1942) – married Mary Elizabeth Anne Layne (1864-1939) in 1887.
2. Mary Elizabeth Jane McConnie (1862-1935) – married John William Gill (1854-1927)
3. Lucretia Cobham McConnie (1864-1939) – married Charles Layne (1863-1940)
4. Samuel Boxill McConnie, Jr. (1866-1956) – unmarried
5. Emily McConnie – unmarried
6. Helen Augusta McConnie (1872-1956) – unmarried
7. Louisa McConnie (1874-??) – no info available.
8. Martha Roscilla McConnie (1877-??) unmarried – (known as Aunt Mattie)
9. Robert William McConnie (1881-1974) – moved to NYC, U.S.A. and married Maude Bloomfield. He changed the spelling of his name to MacConney.
10. Albyn St. Clair McConnie (1885-1974) – married Laurie Marshall (1889-1970) in 1921.

(All above siblings except #8 Martha Roscilla, #9. Robert William and #10. Albyn St.Clair McConnie, were born in Barbados.)

As far as I know, this McConney first family lived in the Ratho Mill area in St. Vincent for many years. My mother always called it Glen. I do not have accurate dates, but I believe that they resided at Ratho Mill for 25-30 years before most of them moved nearer to Kingstown – the capital and seat of the British governing body on the island. With basic infrastructure being established over the years in Kingstown, it had the largest population density in the island, and hence, the best opportunities for laborers, clerks, traders, tradesmen and other service and general workers, to make a living.

While most of the migrating families would have had food and market gardens at Ratho Mill, many of them would likely have tried to maintain trades and skills brought with them to St. Vincent. They did not appear to be poverty-stricken. For example, Samuel Boxill McConnie (1835-1908) was on record as a shopkeeper on his son Richard's baptismal registration in St. Andrew in Barbados in 1860. On Samuel Boxill McConnie's birth registration, his father was listed as a shoemaker, and he and his family were probably the descendants of indentured servants or political exiles brought out from the United Kingdom. In any event, his family had a record of being tradesmen in Barbados.

Then, by deduction, I assume that Samuel Boxill McConnie would have tried to continue making at least part of his livelihood as a shopkeeper in St. Vincent. It is possible (and likely) that he would have tried to sell or barter whatever he could (food, utensils, tools, or services) to the community to sustain the two families he was raising simultaneously. This could probably be done in addition to having their market and vegetable gardens and some livestock to feed the families. As a matter of fact, on his Death Certificate recorded with his date of decease as September 25th, 1908, he was assigned a cause of death as "cardiac syncope" and had his occupation listed as "Planter", a generic term often used for a landowner. His wife, Marianna, died in 1923. Both were buried in the Kingstown Cemetary.

There is evidence of Samuel Boxill McConnie (the father) living at Sion Hill towards the end of his life. His death certificate places him as residing at Sion Hill at the time of his death on

September 25th 1908, listed at age 75, as was reported by Samuel B. McConnie, Jr., his son of the same name (who I will hereafter refer to as Samuel Jr.) It is entirely possible that the hurricane of 1898 that destroyed much of Calliaqua, had something to do with encouraging this move to Sion Hill (not far from Dorsetshire Hill). I have recollections of other cousins (Laynes, Gills and McConnies) living near to the Sion Hill area — at a location known as Frenches, which was not far from Richmond Hill, a location closer to Kingstown.

Here are some notes on Samuel and Marianna McConnie's children:

1. **Richard Alleyne McConnie (1860-1942)**
   He married Mary Elizabeth Layne (1864-1939) and they had nine children (details in chap. 6).

2. **Mary Elizabeth Jane McConnie (1862-1935)**
   She was the second of ten children and was born in Barbados and baptized in St. Andrew on Oct 22nd, 1862. She married John William Gill (1854-1927) and they had six children:
   (A) Gertrude Gill (1883-1964) aka Aunt Gertie
   (B) Otley Leland Gill (1894-1959)
   (C) Dillon Bedford Gill (1897-1967) (married Lilian (Lily) Layne) and had three children – Stuart, Brian & Douglas
   (D) Carlisle McKerith Gill (1898-1970) (married Maisie McConnie) and had three children – Gordon, Janice & Brenton
   (E) Julian Richlea Gill (1900-1983)
   (F) Edward Elvie Elmo Gill (1884-1957) He married Adelaide Holstein and had seven children – Ferdie, Elsie, Ronald, Oriel, Minita, Kathleen and Vernon.

3. **Lucretia (Lulie) Cobham McConnie (1864-1939)**
She was the third of ten children born in Barbados
(Dec. 18, 1864) and was baptized in St.Andrew on
March 23rd, 1865. She married Charles Branford
Layne. They lived at Ratho Mill and had nine
children:
   (A) Ormond Lloyd Layne (1890-??)
   (B) Branford Evelyn Layne (1892-??)
   (C) Clara Roscilla Layne (1893-1907)
   (D) Laurie Alberta Layne (1895-??)
   (E) Elsie Marjorie Layne (1897- ??)
   (F) (Stillborn Child) Layne (1899)
   (G) George Cleveland Layne (1900-??)
   (H) Mary Lucretia Layne (1903-??)
   (I) Lilian Almaida Layne (1905-abt.1957) m.
      Dillon Bedford Gill

4. **Samuel Boxill McConnie, Jr. (1866-1956)**
Samuel, Jr. was born in Barbados (Dec. 30, 1866)
and was baptized on June 2nd 1867. He did not
marry. He was a shoemaker.

5. **Emily McConnie (1868-??)**
She was also known as Emma. She did not marry.

6. **Helen Augusta McConnie (1872-1956)**
She was born in Barbados Nov. 11, 1872 and was
baptized on Feb. 1st, 1873, in St. Andrew. She
moved to St. Vincent with her parents and relocated
to NYC, New York in 1908 where she worked and
died. She never married.

7. **Louisa McConnie (1874-?)**
She was born in Barbados on Dec. 29th, 1874 and
was baptized on April. 3rd 1875. At that time, her
parents lived at Bawden's, St,Andrew. No other info
available.

8. **Martha Roscilla McConnie (1877-??)**
   Born at Gomea, St. Vincent. She did not marry.

9. **William Bowen McConnie (1881-1974)**
   Robert William Bowen McConnie was born in St. Vincent on December 16, 1881. He emigrated to New York and married Maude Bloomfield. They had two children, Walter St.Clair McConnie (1905-1982) who changed the spelling of his family name back to MacConney, and Dorothy Grace McConnie (1906-2009) who never married and worked for the *St.Petersberg Times* for many years.

10. **Albyn St.Clair McConnie (1885-1974)**
    Uncle Mac, as we knew him, was born on Feb. 21st 1885 and lived and died in St. Vincent (Oct. 7, 1974). He married Laurie Marshall on March 12, 1921, and they had one son, Hugh. Hugh married Pat Banfield from Grenada and they had four children: Donna, Wayne, Kurt and Barry. Donna married Gavin McMenigal and had two children, Vernon and Karen, and they live in NZ. Wayne married Dawn Catchpole and they had Jason and Tara. They live in Canada. Kurt married Marie but she died. He then married Mitzi but had no issue. Barry married Julia and had three children, Luke, Oliver and Hanna. Both Kurt and Barry live in the UK.

I would love more information from any credible source to give more detailed on this generation of Barbadian migrants who migrated together and lived in the same community at Ratho Mill, St. Vincent. To start my account of the McConnie progeny that I am more familiar with, I will begin with the eldest in Samuel's first family, Richard Alleyne McConnie and his family in the next chapter.

Reader's Notes

CHAPTER 5

RICHARD ALLEYNE McCONNIE

Richard and his wife, Mary Elizabeth (Liz) Anne (ca. 1930s)

Samuel's eldest son, Richard Alleyne McConnie (1860-1942) was born in Barbados; he was my grandfather. He married Mary Elizabeth Anne Layne (1864-1939) in 1887 in St. Vincent. An official Govt.-issued copy of their marriage certificate confirms this date. Unfortunately, both of my grandparents died before I was born, so my report is second hand. Both were born in Barbados and moved to St. Vincent with their own parents at the ages of 15 and 11 respectively. Twelve years later, they were married at St. Paul's Anglican Church in Calliaqua, St. Vincent (in 1887 at ages 27 and 23 respectively), probably surrounded by their parents, siblings and quite possibly, a motley assortment of the family.

Grandfather Richard Alleyne, according to our cousin Janice (Janice Gill – Maisie's daughter) and confirmed by pictures we received (special thanks to cousins Randy Johnson and Iris Salcedo), was a slim, short man. His wife, my Grandmother Mary Elizabeth Anne, appeared to be of a sturdier build and looked taller than he was. My mother told me she was called Liz or Betty by most people and 'Beauty' by her husband.

Occupations of the McConnie Family:

Grandfather Richard Alleyne McConnie was listed on his marriage certificate as a planter, and Grandmother Mary Elizabeth Anne McConnie (nee Layne), as a seamstress. These job titles were commonly used by the officialdom of the day and offered a somewhat vague idea of their occupations. In all likelihood, they worked very hard physically at many tasks, and, to survive in that era and location, they likely found it difficult to make ends meet financially.

The McConnie family grew their own fruits and ground provisions, and raised livestock and chickens to both sell/barter and feed themselves – perhaps selling off an occasional cow or pig in addition to their produce and providing others with their labor, skills or services – to pay for clothing, shelter and everyday living expenses. Barter was very common in those days, as it was a most practical method for obtaining goods or services without resorting to scarce cash. Judging by their children's lifestyles (my aunts and uncles), the family must have been thrifty spenders.

I am not familiar with the early lifestyle or even the details of the livelihood of Richard Alleyne and his wife, Mary Elizabeth Anne. I knew they kept a large kitchen garden in Kingstown where they raised ground provisions, breadfruit and cocoa, as well as mangoes, sugar apples, sorrel, peas, limes and guavas. They raised chickens and spent buckets of time chasing neighborhood dogs and other predatory animals from their backyard. In particular, I recall a feud they had with a neighbor whose pig occasionally got out of his pen and rooted around on their property. It was the closest I ever saw my Aunt Lynn (Dora Alinda) come to a pitched battle (only words, thankfully) with the neighbor. From stories I vaguely recall hearing, they had an active family life, and I experienced their celebrations of all religious holidays with a large meal.

I recall being told not only of their love of family but also their focus on helping their children get ahead. I understand from my father (Alick Nanton) that both McConnie sons, Richard Cleve and Julian, attended the St. Vincent Agricultural School for some period of their school days. Fortunately, I have been able to find, and have been given, photos of Richard Alleyne and Mary Elizabeth Anne and their young family from both my mother as well as from family members. Using these pictures, I have tried to piece together some aspects of their lives as the family grew, but research cannot not always provide a good look at the "big picture." So, bear with me as I present what I have gathered along the way.

Richard Alleyne McConnie, after moving the family to Kingstown – Murray's Rd. area (which I place around 1910) – owned and managed a small one-door retail cloth store. I have never discovered if Richard Alleyne started it himself or purchased it. The store, as I knew it, was called *The Central Store* until it was closed (or sold) in or around 1960. *The Central Store* was located in the heart of the business district of Kingstown. It opened onto a secondary street aptly named Middle Street. Middle Street had a cobblestone surface that could jar the back teeth of a bike rider in a rush. This street was filled with literally thousands of people who came to town on Saturdays to sell their wares or purchase foodstuffs, clothing or other items for their families. You would literally have to jostle your way through these crowds to move around.

I was aware that in the 1950s, when I lived in Kingstown, that the unmarried daughters, Aunt Lynn (Dora Alinda) and Aunt Cill (Cecily Ermine), both worked at *The Central Store* retailing cloth cut from bolts to support themselves and Auntie B (Betha Idalie). Auntie B did all the housekeeping and cooking at home. These sister-spinsters had some limited help from a housemaid I knew as Millie.

My grandmother, Mary Elizabeth Anne McConnie, was listed as a seamstress on her marriage certificate. She acquired the skill of sewing perhaps from her mother or some family member or friend. As all clothing and shoes were hand-made at the time, it was a useful and probably a valuable occupation when she was asked to make clothing for others. She passed on her skills of sewing, knitting, crocheting, and tatting (a durable lace used for centerpieces and edging for dresses, etc.) to all her daughters.

I recall that Aunt Cill (Cecily Ermine) and my mother, (Ada Elaine), were adept at knitting and crochet (it seemed to take months to crochet a complete tablecloth or bed covering). The other sisters were also skilled at sewing, darning and embroidery – as they had to keep their clothing in good repair. I also recall that Aunt Cill loved tatting, (a process of winding, looping and knotting threads) which seemed to require even more patience than crocheting to complete. While most of the sisters would have learned to sew and knit of necessity, Auntie 'B' (Betha Idalie) developed a lasting reputation as a fine seamstress who made wedding dresses, baptismal gowns and decorative dresses.

CHAPTER 6

RICHARD ALLEYNE & MARY ELIZABETH ANNE McCONNIE'S FAMILY

Richard Alleyne McConnie (1860-1942), my grandfather, married Mary Elizabeth Anne Layne (1864-1939) on Feb. 17th, 1887. They had nine children at Ratho Mill in an 18-year period:

1. **Dora Alinda McConnie (1888-1959) unmarried – (Aunt Lynn)**
2. **Richard Cleve McConnie (1890-1949) – Uncle Cleve m. Iris King (1899-1985)**
3. **Betha Idalie McConnie (1893-1970) unmarried – (who we knew as: 'Auntie B')**
4. **Julian O'Cara McConnie (1894-1947) – (Uncle Julian m. Marina Sandoz)**
5. **Cecily Ermine McConnie (1896-1972) unmarried – (Aunt Cill)**
6. **Stella Lavinia McConnie (1898-1984) – (Aunt Stella m. Arthur Gill)**
7. **Mary Olive Louise McConnie (1901-1965) – (Aunt Maisie m. Lisle Gill)**
8. **Ernest Norbert McConnie (1903-1904) – (died as an infant at 10 mos. old)**
9. **Ada Elaine McConnie (1906-1990) – (m. W.A.G. [Alick] Nanton)**

I have guestimated that, prior to moving to 'town' (Kingstown, the capital), the family had lived at Glen (Ratho Mill) in the country for about 25+ years. Some records and family members relayed that Richard Alleyne was a shopkeeper as well as a planter, a combination which may have helped him financially with his move from the country into 'town' and to buy a house there. He almost certainly was a key player in the small, family dry goods store that became *The Central Store*, and probably started it. As close as I can ascertain, Richard Alleyne McConnie moved his family to Kingstown from Ratho Mill sometime between 1906 and 1920. They moved to *Clover Mead*, a house on Murray's Road on the outskirts of Kingstown, the capital, opposite to the existing Girls High School. His surviving children occupied that house until 1967, when it was sold for commercial use (as a political party headquarters). The values that the family held dear were their (Anglican) religion, hard work and determination to get ahead, as well as the education of their children. No slackers there!

The house the family lived in on Murray's Road was a wooden structure with exterior cedar shakes on the external walls (painted white), and glass sash windows fitted on either side with jalousie louvres to allow any breezes blowing to circulate during the hot days and nights. For sleeping arrangements, I recall the house in the 1950s having three specific bedrooms and two other adjacent smaller rooms, once used as bedrooms, for this large family. These last two rooms were converted to sitting and changing rooms in later years. I also recall indoor plumbing, an indoor water closet, a large, deep concrete bath, a pantry, and a dining room with an adjacent attached outdoor kitchen. There was also an exterior traditional outhouse used by both family and hired help.

Growing up (in the 1950s and '60s), I recall their house had electricity that was probably wired in the 1930s by their cousin, Dillon Bedford Gill. I remember those old brass/ceramic/Bakelite switches and outlets, bayonet light bulbs, wired fuses, etc., but no telephone – which was a luxury they couldn't afford. Deserving special mention were the many locks, carriage bolts and latches to deter burglars on every window and door. When I spent time there as a boy, burglaries were common in Kingstown, and every house was locked up tight at night.

This will not be news, but all the McConnies had good appetites (including a 'sweet tooth') and none of them appeared undernourished in the 1950s and 1960s when I was growing up. This made for good cooks and methods for storing foods and foodstuffs. For the record, cooking in the islands pre-1940 was done on open fires and coal pots – iron pots filled with charcoal for cooking. Coal pots were supplemented by open-fire cooking when the family pot was too large to fit on a coal pot (e.g., if making soup for a large number). The kerosene stove (invented in 1892) did not come into use in St. Vincent until around the 1940s, and they were a fire hazard when not used and maintained safely in the wooden houses of the day.

The kerosene refrigerator – which followed the ice box – was not invented until the 1920s. (Kerosene refrigerators could actually make ice cubes – you would fill the ice cube trays every night with water and hoped they would freeze overnight.) Kerosene appliances were efficient but had a kerosene odor and needed to be monitored for safety reasons, especially when you were refilling them with kerosene fuel indoors. I do not know if the McConnie family acquired kerosene appliances before 1945. Perhaps some family member reading this account might know more of the family's lifestyle in Kingstown between 1910 to 1940, a period in which I have had to use records to reconstruct.

At the back of the McConnie house, there was a semi-enclosed outdoor kitchen area adjoining the house for open fires and coal-pot cooking. There was a large backyard where they had planted a few cocoa, coconut and breadfruit trees, a mango tree where their chickens roosted, an avocado tree, as well as a soursop, a sugar apple, and some guava fruit trees. I also recall picking limes and digging up shallots (spring onions). They used itinerant labor in the 1950s to plant root crops/ground provisions and vegetables at the very back portion of their land – including sweet potatoes, dashene, tannias, yams and sweet potatoes. Other food crops they planted from time to time included pigeon peas, split peas, hot peppers, ginger, and callaloo. These were not cultivated simultaneously, but as my aunts grew older, only when itinerant labor became available.

The diet of the McConnies always included ground provisions, peas or beans, rice, and some meat – which was more expensive to serve. Their most memorable meals in which we were included from time to time were the occasional Sunday main meal, and more frequently, holiday meals (esp. Easter and Christmas). They made lemonade drinks and occasionally, a sorrel drink. These fruit drinks always tasted better than soda drinks (which were known as sweet drinks). Then there was their "Rice wine" which they made with rice, oranges, limes, prunes, egg whites and shells, yeast, sugar, and water. It had the taste of a dessert wine. (...and they did not become 'Moonshiners.') I have salvaged that recipe from my mother's handwritten notes and it is reproduced in Appendix B (p.127).

In pre-refrigeration days, animals and fowls had to be slaughtered and cleaned for the table for immediate use, and the McConnie family would use local (domestic) help for some of those tasks. I certainly recall the chase to catch fowls with my aunts and hired help, and the resulting plucking, cleaning and cooking before being placed on the table as a tasty-cooked chicken. Roosters, who were more feisty, seemed hardest to catch, and there was some plotting and planning that went into chasing and catching them to have them prepared for the dinner table. They had no chicken coops; the fowls were free-range chickens, and the hens were encouraged to nest near the outdoor kitchen in straw-filled areas of the covered storage area that was checked daily for eggs. Some fowls inevitably wandered off, and some were stolen or were eaten by dogs. Aunts Lynn, Betha or Cill could often be found at dusk feeding the fowls and then 'shooing' them up into the backyard trees to keep them safe from predators – usually the neighborhood dogs prowling for food. Thankfully, there were no poisonous snakes in St. Vincent.

The front entrance to the McConnie house in Kingstown was planted with decorative ferns and flowering plants – they loved roses and orchids – and there was a narrow groomed path that led from the access road to the front staircase. The staircase opened unto a railed verandah. The verandah roof was about six-foot wide as you entered via the front entrance gate from the front steps and led to a more spacious covered sitting area (perhaps 10ft x 15ft) on the side (facing *Shamrock*, the Layne residence next door), which gave access to the front door of the house. The gallery was bounded by a sturdy top rail supported by X-crossed supports (one by twos) in a repeat pattern that enclosed the gallery. The fascia at the roofline was decorated with a ginger-bread fretwork typical of Victorian architecture.

The house was about three to four feet above ground level and the adjoining verandah was built as a covered balcony where you could sit out of the direct rays of the sun. There was often a light breeze and the raised verandah commanded a good view of the main road. All grassed lawn areas and drainage swales were cut by hand, using hired labor (machetes were wielded to cut the grass and shrub weeds), and could look manicured, depending on the care taken to cut it on each occasion. To my recollection, their land area was about three-quarters of an acre in size.

In time, five of the McConnie siblings got married and had children, and the remaining three sisters were spinsters who lived there all or most of their lives. The spinsters were Dora Alinda (Aunt Lynn), Betha Idalie (Auntie B) and Cecily Ermine (Aunt Cill). They lived in the above-described family home on Murray's Rd with their parents – both of whom who passed away before I was born – Granny Mary Elizabeth Ann in 1939 and Grandad Richard Alleyne McConnie in 1942). Aunt Lynn, Auntie B and Aunt Cill, the spinsters, continued to live there.

After Aunt Lynn died in 1959, the other two remained in this family house until 1967, when they were taken by Ada and Alick (Geoff's parents) to Barbados to live out their lives. Barbados offered better medical facilities as well as the availability of specialized doctors. They moved to Barbados and lived at *Ridgeway* in Ventnor Terrace, Ch.Ch., until both sisters, Betha and Cecily, passed away in 1970 and 1972 respectively. Alec and Ada then moved to Florida with Geoff and Helen in 1980 to be close to their children (Jennifer lived in Vero Beach, FL and Mac lived in Ontario, Canada at that time) and their grandchildren.

As you can imagine, on St. Vincent, an island with meagre resources, the McConnie clan had to be self-reliant. There were very few grocers in town, so many itinerant hucksters plied their trade up through the 1950s. At that time, the family ate their own home-raised (and skinned and plucked) chickens and home-grown ground provisions and fruit. Fish and meat were purchased from itinerant hucksters. I recall Aunt Cill (Cecily Ermine) churning a whipped white butter in a mason jar from the cream skimmed off the milk daily – delivered on the head of a courier from miles away in the country (in a milk can that probably held five gallons). I also recall Dad helping them 'cure' a ham (from a leg of pork) in the 1950s from time to time. In my youth (1950s/60s), I recall Auntie B (Betha Idalie) and the maid cooked meals of chicken or fish, breadfruit, rice, pigeon peas, plantains and ground provisions.[5]

The Aunts' "Rice Wine"[6] was the sweet dessert wine that was served on high days and holidays. We were usually offered a glass as kids and enjoyed it even though we never felt we had enough. (No, none of us turned out to be alcoholics!)

In the next section, we move on to the individual family members (the siblings) in birth order. I trust this will give some

---

5. Ground provisions refer to root crops like sweet potatoes, dashene, yams and eddoes.

6. Recipe for Rice Wine is included at the end of this writing (Appendix B).

chronological order to the study, as the time frame over which it is written spans close to 150 years (1875 to 2025). Each immediate family member is given their own section and as much material as I could recall or locate in any existing writings or records.

The internet has also been of great use in developing the information presented – particularly for family members who travelled to the USA. The ship's manifests archived on Ellis island, the genealogical websites and the U.S. city and state records were invaluable in helping to fix dates in many family member's major moves and events.

The local records in Barbados were also very useful. Unfortunately, the records in St. Vincent are less accessible, and information recorded in St. Vincent was often destroyed by hurricanes, fires or poor storage in the high humidity that exists there. However, there are still many hard-copy archival records housed there in the Office of the Archives.

FAMILY PORTRAIT
of
RICHARD ALLEYNE &
MARY ELIZABETH ANNE
McCONNIE & THEIR GIRLS
(Circa 1915)

Dora Alinda

Betha Idalie

Cecily Ermine

Mary Olive Louise
(Maisie)

Stella
Lavinia

Richard Alleyne

Mary Elizabeth Anne
(Liz)

Ada Elaine

Richard & Liz McConnie
and the girls - ca.1915

CHAPTER 7

DORA ALINDA McCONNIE
(1888-1959)

The eldest of Richard Alleyne and Mary Elizabeth Anne's children was Dora Alinda McConnie – I knew her as Aunt Lynn. As I was ten years old when she died of a diabetic condition (gangrene of the toe), my personal knowledge of her in her youth and middle age is limited to what I remember from my mother, Ada, her youngest sister. Aunt Lynn was the eldest child in the family, and I do recall that, after her parents both passed on, she took on the household leadership role for personal, family or business-related challenges and ruled with an iron fist. If there was a difference of opinion at the small dry goods store that she and her sister Cecily ran *(The Central Store)*, she would handle the person(s) or problem(s) with a spirited offence and, as far as I knew, peace would reign again. I am guessing that Grandad Richard Alleyne was involved in starting and running *The Central Store* earlier (1910s to 1940s) after he moved his family into town (which I date somewhere between 1906 and 1910). I never thought of asking my mother or her sisters about the date of their move. While this was of little or no importance to me at the time, children of that era were not encouraged to ask too many questions; I guess it was considered impolite.

Aunt Lynn was as religious as her parents and siblings, and she never missed a church service or her offerings to the church. She enjoyed chatting with the minister at the Cathedral after a service and often invited them to come for a meal. In fact, she had a cousin, Fred Layne, who was an Anglican minister and often visited with the McConnie family. [Uncle Fred remained close to our family and baptized our eldest son, Andrew, in Barbados when we lived there in 1978.]

The Central Store was a small family-owned dry goods store that sold cloth (cut from large bolts of cloth) by the yard. As far as I know, it was a family business, and the sisters shared in the proceeds when there were profits beyond their expenses, if any. Interestingly, it seemed to me that they only hired clerks from Dorsetshire Hill who descended from the migrants who came from Barbados. I recall clerks at different times with names like Miss Gabriel, Miss Gooding, and Miss Bradshaw. (That was what I called them, and I never knew if they were single or married, if they had children, significant others, or other family members).

Of some small interest, I do recall that this small store did a brisk trade in brightly-patterned headscarf cloth for women, usually on Saturdays, and in December in the two weeks before Christmas. Also, as cloth was only sold by the yard, and there were no ready-made clothes available, seamstresses and tailors were in great demand (as were shoemakers). In fact, most women had to sew their own clothes as well as clothes for family members.

I have memories of Aunt Lynn, Auntie B and Aunt Cill living in the McConnie family home in my youth at Murray's Road just outside of the capital, Kingstown in the 1950s and 1960s. I recall that whenever their neighbor allowed his pig to wander over onto their land, Aunt Lynn would shout at him in a stentorian voice (for intimidation purposes), and demand he remove his pig that was eating their ground provisions and other crops on their land, generally rooting around and turning their back yard into a mushy pigsty. Aunt Lynn, the eldest sibling, was a no-nonsense person and (verbal) protector of her sisters. She was known as a person who 'called a spade a shovel' – no messing around. When walking to work with Aunt Cill, they both ALWAYS carried an umbrella in case of the normal sudden, torrential, drenching showers and thunderstorms. In fact, most of the folk walking to work would have needed an umbrella. These umbrellas doubled as a sunshade in hot, sunny weather.

Aunt Lynn was always very kind to us kids, but was not one for much small talk, and she liked being on the move. Like her parents, she was focused, industrious and forward looking, a planner. Unfortunately, she became a diabetic in her later years, and, after having her gangrenous toe removed, did not survive but for a few days. She passed away at the age of 71 in St. Vincent.

*Reader's Notes*_____

_____

_____

_____

_____

_____

CHAPTER 8

RICHARD CLEVE McCONNIE

(1890-1949)

Richard Cleve McConnie was the second child and eldest son in the family. My dad (Alick Nanton) told me that Richard and his younger brother Julian both attended the St. Vincent Agricultural School in Kingstown, the capital. If this information is correct, the Richard Alleyne McConnie family may have been prompted to move to Kingstown from Calliaqua to allow them to attend that school, as they would not have been able to walk the approximately five to six mile distance every school day between Ratho Mill and Kingstown – especially when the only way to commute would have been on foot in a very hot and rainy climate with frequent thunder storms (the lightning was epic). Moving into the town would also have allowed granddad Richard Alleyne to open and operate *The Central Store* – his small retail dry goods store.

For transportation on the island in the early 1900s, there were horse-drawn carriages and donkey carts and probably precious few automobiles, if any. Bicycles and motorcycles would have followed around the 1920s, if not sooner. At the time, there was an assortment of bicycles in Europe, including the 'penny-farthing' with its two vastly different-sized wheels. Richard Cleve's father may well have had a bicycle of some kind to take him to work. However, the McConnie daughters who worked with him would have had to walk, as girls did not ride bicycles in those days. A walk of several miles (three to five miles) was not uncommon to go to school, church, or work in those times. I remember walking perhaps three to four miles to go to church on Sundays until our mother had a car to drive us there.[7] For walking around, members of the family carried large umbrellas everywhere – shading them from the hot sun and providing shelter from the frequent drenching rain.

Uncle Richard Cleve (aka Cleve by his family in St. Vincent), attended the St. Vincent Agricultural School to learn Agronomy as well as other liberal arts. Mixed in with education on agriculture, the students were taught Mathematics, History and English Grammar, as well as other subjects including art and music instruction. His daughter, Iris, stated that he also learned to play the violin there. The Agricultural School only operated from 1900 to around 1913/14 and took in students from the age of 8 years old. This school was superseded by a new Boys Grammar School (founded in 1908), and the St. Vincent Agricultural School was closed by 1914. At that point in time, the new Boys Grammar School took over the Agricultural School's premises and very likely its remaining student body.

On a handwritten note in a notebook dating back to 1930, Ada wrote that "Cleve went to Pembroke, 22nd March 1909." Pembroke was a sugar cane-growing estate in the south-west of the island – also known locally as 'down Leeward' – and this was likely his initiation into actual agricultural work. This was probably where he had the accident that damaged his knee. As per Sister (Iris Blanche), his only daughter, Uncle Cleve had an unfortunate accident as a teenager (he would have been 19 in 1909) while driving a tractor in St. Vincent as a teenager. The tractor apparently tipped over on uneven ground on top of him, and

---

7. Walking was the mode of transport for the poor Vincentian of that day. It was not unusual for students or poor people to walk 2 to 4 miles per day.

he luckily escaped with only an injured knee. The affected knee never healed properly over the remainder of his life. He used a cane thereafter, but was still able to ride a horse capably at his job in Puerto Rico, and his daughter 'Sister' told us that he dressed his damaged knee every day of his life thereafter.

At 21 years old, Uncle Cleve left St. Vincent for New York in 1911 "to seek his fortune." My mother recorded his departure date as August 7, 1911. Family reports handed down tell us that he started working with a restaurant in New York City. Per his daughter Iris (aka 'Sister'), one day while working there, he overheard a conversation with a customer he was serving. The man told his dinner companion at his table that he was looking for help on a sugar plantation in Puerto Rico. Cleve then told the gentleman, Mr. Bass (General Manager of the Fajardo Sugar Company), that he was familiar with the sugar industry, having worked in agriculture previously. This was a fortuitous conversation, and one which led to his getting a job with the Fajardo Sugar Company in Puerto Rico. With his agricultural background to help him, including his studying Agronomy in St. Vincent, he enjoyed long-term successful employment with this company.

In addition to his success in Puerto Rico, and perhaps because he was the eldest son of a responsible and industrious family, he became somewhat of a patriarch for his own family as well as his wife's. He first returned home to St. Vincent 'on leave' and spent two weeks (July 15th to Aug. 1st) in 1915. From both my mother's comments and that of his daughter 'Sister', he frequently sent home funds to St. Vincent on a regular basis to help both his parents and siblings.

Richard Cleve married Iris Beryl King (1899–1985) on September 18th, 1917. She was the daughter of a Barbadian, Joseph B. King, who also worked in Puerto Rico on a neighboring sugar plantation. After he was married (Sept. 18th, 1917), Richard Cleve subsequently set up his father-in-law in business on a small sugar estate in Barbados (Haggett's Plantation).

Cleve and Iris had four children – Richard Lionel, Randolph Joseph, Iris Blanche ('Sister'), and Ralph O'Cara. He had a successful career with the Fajardo Sugar Company and sent his children to college. They all graduated and details follow below.

Perhaps one of my most interesting discoveries in Uncle Cleve's career was that he became a sugar scientist of note. He recorded his observations and results from his sugar cane field experiments and was quoted in research papers in the sugar industry. I tracked his research papers from 1913 through 1932 (and they may well go further into his career). In my internet research, I noted that he was quoted and referenced in multiple research papers. According to his daughter, Iris Blanche McConnie (who clued me in to his scientific side), he also traveled to sugar-growing areas including Hawaii, Haiti and Louisiana to widen his knowledge and improve his research of the product. The papers he wrote or co-wrote centered on entomology and soils, as well as on his findings on strains of sugar cane plants that were immune to disease. In addition to his position of Field Supervisor for Fajardo Sugar, he conducted his R & D there as well. In this capacity, he managed test acreages on a portion of the Fajardo sugar holdings that were fully committed to research and development.

With early success in the agricultural industry in Puerto Rico, he persuaded his brother Julian, also schooled in Agronomy in St. Vincent, to join him in Puerto Rico some four years after he arrived at Fajardo. He also helped him find a job in the Puerto Rican sugar industry with another subsidiary of the Fajardo Sugar Company. In my mother's records, Cleve, his wife, Iris Beryl, and son (baby Richard), visited with his parents in St. Vincent for ten days (Aug. 7th to 17th) in 1919 – probably to show them his wife and their first grandson. From my mother's notes, the last trip he made with his wife and four children to St. Vincent stated that they arrived on July 10th 1929. No other details were noted.

Uncle Cleve also helped his sisters (Stella and Mary Olive Louise/ Maisie) to migrate to the USA in order to get them on their feet financially. In addition, he made a very generous offer to his youngest sister (my mother), Ada Elaine. She was 16 years his junior and had excelled academically in St. Vincent. He offered to send her to the United States to study Law – a field she was interested in, but this offer she never pursued. I suspect that Ada, adventurous though she was, may have had competing interests that were more important to her at the time. Maybe it was a case of boyfriends? ...ageing parents? ...her job at the Govt. Post Office where she made money and could help the family? Any of these may have overridden her desire to travel to the U.S.A. to study. In this case, I always felt my mother, Ada, never allowed herself to fulfill her academic dreams.

Uncle Cleve, faithful to his family values, was a true believer in education, sending two of his children (Richard and Randy) to Cornell University, and his daughter Iris attended both boarding school and Goucher College (at the time Goucher was a gateway to Johns Hopkins when she was considering studying medicine). Ralph, Cleve's youngest son, attended the University of Puerto Rico on the G.I. Bill, and went on to study optometry. Richard Cleve certainly attained great success with his career and family. Unfortunately, he passed away at a relatively young 59 years of age because of a heart condition.

Richard Cleve McConnie

CHAPTER 9

BETHA IDALIE McCONNIE
(1893-1970)

Betha (also known as 'Auntie B' by her nieces and nephews) was the third child of Richard Alleyne and Mary Elizabeth Anne McConnie. (Her name was NOT Bertha as some genealogists assume.) She was one of the three spinster aunts that we knew while growing up. My siblings (Mac & Jen) and I spent occasional weekends and holidays at their house. We were always well fed and never left their house without one treat or another. Our treats varied – they could be a single candy, a threepenny coin (known as thruppence), or even fruit from their garden (such as a mango, or a pawpaw as we called it then – a papaya). They loved us unreservedly.

Auntie B was a quiet person. She had made a distinct impression with her sewing and knitting skills with her family, relatives and friends. She made decorative wedding and other special dresses along with christening gowns for infants. As an accomplished dressmaker, she made fancy dresses and decorated them with crochet, tatting and lace (according to my mother). In later life, she was an excellent cook – and took responsibility for cooking for her sisters (Lynn & Cill) every day when they came home from work. She also excelled in making 'rice wine' and 'coconut sugar cakes' as well as taking charge of the cooking for family gatherings they hosted. We loved eating there and enjoying her cooking.

27.7.31.

This is how I looked
at the wedding.

For Iris with love
from Bettie.

Betha Idalie McConnie (1931)
Taken outside the family home at Murray's Rd, Kingstown

I was told that Auntie B was a very attractive young lady in her youth (and verified by the picture dated and signed by her above in 1931). However, I suspect that living in an era when she was restricted by both her parents and society, not to mention having to help with the upkeep of the house and other domestic chores, she never found a husband. I believe she lived a quiet life as she aged. I recall she went out infrequently and enjoyed cooking, sewing and a lifestyle to which they had become accustomed on their small plot of land. As she aged, she was not a complainer, but would mention cramping muscles from time to time as she got older. Auntie B adopted the role of the family homemaker from her mother. After her mother's passing, she took full responsibility for the cooking and cleaning for the family, including her father and her two unmarried sisters who resided in the family home.

In her younger days, during the 20s and 30s, family get-togethers were popular, and a trip to a riverside or to a beach perhaps by bus or horse-drawn wagon (walking was another distinct possibility) was a great opportunity for a picnic and a change of pace from the usual home chores. That was the excitement of the day. Socializing at these 'outings' as they were called, was a major part of life enjoyment for sedate ladies and families. At least, these were events that were considered safe to attend and talk about, whatever else went on.

Auntie B was of an even temperament and, though not an adventurer, she found satisfaction in taking care of her sisters and herself and the home. As she got to a more advanced age (74), she and her sister Cill (Cecily), both accompanied their youngest sister, Ada, to Barbados to live out her last three years there. Ada and Alick were able to look after them and make them comfortable there until they passed. Auntie B passed away at the age of 77, after a life essentially of hard work and was buried in Barbados. She gave unstintingly of herself throughout her life to both her family and her sewing skills.

*Reader's Notes*_____

_____

_____

_____

_____

_____

CHAPTER 10

JULIAN O'CARA McCONNIE
(1894-1947)

Uncle Julian was the fourth child and the second of two boys in the McConnie family. Again, my knowledge of Uncle Julian is second-hand as I never met him. In travels to Puerto Rico in the 1970s, I met many of his family briefly. If any of his family should choose to contact me, I would love to obtain more information on him for posterity, as I plan to circulate this information to members of the family, some of whom may have an interest in the St. Vincent McConnie family roots.

According to my Dad (Alick), Uncle Julian attended the St. Vincent Agricultural School (just as his brother, Richard Cleve, had done). Recently corroborated by my mother's records, he started at this school on Jan. 20th, 1910. Being four years younger than his brother Richard Cleve, he remained with his parents in St. Vincent until Cleve invited him to come to join him in Puerto Rico to work in the sugar industry. It is likely that he worked in the agricultural industry for a brief period in St. Vincent. However, his future in St. Vincent would probably have been very limited, and as a youngster, he would have been willing to move in order to achieve a better and more exciting future than he could have enjoyed in the St. Vincent of that day. Cleve's visit back to St. Vincent in July 1915, and no doubt his description of the opportunities available in Puerto Rico likely spurred Julian on to migrate there in late 1915.

I do not have a lot of information on Julian's life in St. Vincent. I do have a picture of him with the rest of his family) that I have dated around 1914 (not a confirmed date, the actual date may be different). Could this have been a family picture that his parents wished to have as a record of the whole family (not including Cleve), before Uncle Julian left home? Who knows? This will probably never be known.

Leaving one's family, even for greener pastures, is difficult, but the thought of adventure and progress to come are a huge draw – as I discovered when I left St. Vincent many years later in 1966 to seek my own future. So, as planned Uncle Julian left in 1915 for Puerto Rico. His name was recorded in the ship's manifest (the Motor Schooner *CREOLE*) that took him to Puerto Rico. The date on the manifest was Dec. 1st, 1915. His parents were both in their early 50s at that point in time, and I am sure they were saddened to lose their second son departing for a life unknown, but simultaneously pleased to think his future would be better than the one he would have had in an economically-challenged St. Vincent, not to mention that he would be with his brother in Puerto Rico.

Uncle Julian worked with a subsidiary of the Fajardo Sugar Company initially, and married Marina Sandoz on Sept. 20th, 1919. They started a family and decided to move to Cuba (late 1920s or early 1930s) for him to obtain further advancement in his sugar industry career. Julian and his family stayed only a short time in Cuba, as he was not comfortable with the activities of the dictatorial Fulgencio Batista regime. He left Cuba in 1932 to return to Puerto Rico. Back in Puerto Rico with his family, he returned to the sugar industry and worked with the Eastern Sugar Corp. in Caguas.

I have found records of Uncle Julian traveling to NYC as well as a WWII Draft Registration card, but no other salient information to record. If any of his relatives wish to supply this information, I would love to have it to complete this vignette of Uncle Julian. He passed away in 1947 of a heart attack, leaving his wife, Marina and his three children (Paul, Julian and Betty). Unfortunately, I have no record of his visiting his parents after he left in 1915.

From information supplied by Randy and Iris Murray (his nephew and niece), Uncle Julian was a family man and he and his brother Richard Cleve remained closely connected throughout their lives in Puerto Rico. Julian maintained a close kinship with his niece Iris (Sister, as she was known), and taught her to ride. The brothers had their children spend time with each other during vacations – so the families got to know each other well – and they spent Thanksgivings and Christmases together as well. These were solid indicators of close-knit family.

So here was the history of another industrious McConnie. Uncle Julian passed away at 53 years of age in 1947, also due to a heart condition.

*Reader's Notes*_____

_____

_____

_____

_____

_____

CHAPTER 11

CECILY ERMINE McCONNIE
(1896-1972)

Cecily Ermine McConnie, (who I knew as Aunt Cill), was the fifth child of Richard Alleyne and Mary Elizabeth Anne McConnie. She was a quiet, gentle, and timid but determined soul. She was always willing to help in any way she could. I know very little of her as a young person and can only speculate from knowing her late in life that she was a quiet homebody. She never married and I don't know who her circle of friends would have been outside of relatives, family and from church.

I knew Aunt Cill as a boy growing up; she was in her late fifties/ early sixties and had a very caring mentality. My brother, Mac, my sister, Jen, and I would spend weekends with the aunts (Alinda, Betha and Cecily). I also spent time with them when my parents and siblings were travelling and left me with them.

When Aunt Cill was my babysitter, she would talk to me about the family and keep an eye on me to be sure I stayed out of mischief (very difficult). I think I was a bright spot at that time in her otherwise quiet (dreary?) life. She tried to interest me in her Bible reading, but at seven or eight years old, I was not much interested. I did, however, love to be with her as she was gentle and made much of me whenever I spent time with herself and her two sisters at the family home.

As mentioned earlier, I remember Aunt Cill churning butter from milk cream in her favorite rocking chair. Milk was delivered on the head of a courier (often a boy or girl from the country) in a metal milk container. The milk was first boiled and then left to cool. The cream that rose to the surface was skimmed off daily for making butter. Aunt Cill would take a mason jar holding between one and two quarts, add a sprinkle of salt and shake it back and forth (churning) for what seemed like hours. She did all of this churning in a rocking chair. When finished, she would pour off the water and the butter left was like a white cream. Her family used it instead of table butter and I remember using it to butter the "penny loaves" that were commonly purchased by everyone there at the time. (The penny loaf was about 7" long with cone-like ends and a crusty surface.) For baking, cakes and pastry goods were made mostly using margarine.

Aunt Cill worked at the small family store, *The Central Store* in Middle Street, Kingstown. Like most smaller stores in Kingstown, it had a double door entrance and two glass windows on either side of the door at the front of the store. When closing the store, the lock up utilized a long flat iron bar that crossed the double door exterior and was secured by protruding pins with locks through them. The windows used a similar arrangement – they were hinged wooden panels that covered the glass windows. These had external diagonal iron bars that were secured from the inside. The irons had a bolt inserted through the iron bar on the outside and secured with small flat iron pins threaded through the incoming bolt on the inside. They were considered burglar proof, although there were several cases of burglary in Kingstown that I recall, but none to *The Central Store* of which I was aware.

The Central Store sold mostly cloth goods. There were cotton, gabardine, wool, seersucker and who-knows-what-other bolts of cloth and lacy materials of many varieties. I recall some that were specifically sold for head wraps/scarves. The bolts of cloth were purchased from visiting salesmen and through local agents. I recall that Aunt Stella also sent goods down from New York from time to time to sell at the store, as there was not much available to purchase locally to resell in a dry goods store.

All businesses in the 1940s, 1950s and 1960s, including *The Central Store* in St. Vincent, worked six days a week, working a halfday only on Wednesdays and Saturdays, except for holidays when businesses were not opened. They worked longer hours in December, especially near Christmas time, when most stores in Kingstown (the capital) opened longer. Aunt Cill mainly worked as the cashier for the store (there were usually two or three clerks hired from the Dorsetshire Hill area, along with Aunts Lynn and Cill who operated the store), but Aunt Lynn was the driver of the business who kept it going. The sisters, Aunts Lynn and Cill, walked two miles to and from work every day. They never owned a car and were always accompanied by their 'signature' umbrellas to shield themselves from the hot sun and the frequent rains.

Aunt Cill did not cook for the sisters, that was Auntie B's (Betha's) bailiwick as the homemaker. Aunt Cill spent much of her home time helping out with chores; and when not helping around the house, in her very little spare time, she could be found reading, sewing, doing crochet and tatting. While some items could take years to complete, she made shawls, tablecloths, doilies, and other items used in the home for relatives and friends. They might be given for wedding gifts or celebration gifts, as every family of that era had some of these treasured items.

Aunt Cill had trouble with her eyes. She worked until she was around 60 years old. She lost her vision in both eyes around 1960. My mother took her to Trinidad to have surgery on her eyes – for detached retinas. We were told that the surgery progressed well, and she was sent home and placed on bed rest. Six to eight weeks later, she became tired of not doing anything at home, and went down to the Cathedral to clean and weed her mother's grave. She apparently bent over to weed and, because the surgery on her eyes had not healed, the retinas in both eyes were affected and were pronounced permanently detached by a local optometrist. She now became blind. An English lady working with the Institute for the Blind in St. Vincent tried to teach her braille. She tried but was unable to master braille. So, she spent most of the rest of her life doing what little she could do to look after herself and not be a burden to anyone. She never complained; she was accustomed to living a life without many comforts, and enjoyed talking to her close family and friends who visited her – some of whom would also read to her.

Aunt Cill's last days were spent with her sister, Ada, in Barbados. As mentioned previously, Aunt Cill and Auntie B moved with Alick and Ada to Ventnor Terrace in Rockley, Ch.Ch. in 1967. Aunt Cill passed away in 1972 at 76 years of age and was buried in Barbados.

*Reader's Notes*_____

_____

_____

_____

_____

_____

CHAPTER 12

STELLA LAVINIA McCONNIE
(1898-1984)

Taking a direct quote from her granddaughter, Carol, "She loved her family fiercely!" Aunt Stella was adventurous, industrious and forthright. Like all of her siblings, I knew little of her in her youth. As I met her and got to know her much later in her life, I enjoyed her direct and unabashed method of speaking. She was the sixth child in this large family of nine (one of whom, Ernest Norbert, died very early in childhood). What I was told about her was that she was taught sewing as a girl at home, and she loved flowers and gardening. In fact, I do recall that all the sisters loved gardening and flowers, and they grew and tended many beautiful flowers wherever they lived.

In her twenties, Stella sailed to NYC in April 1922 on the *S.S. VESTRIS*, going through Ellis Island, NY, and was accompanied by cousins from St. Vincent – Dillon, Carlisle and Julian Gill – as well as by Alick (dad). Coincidentally, they were all on their way to New York. I have often wondered if they planned to travel together. Aunt Stella declared on the manifest of the *VESTRIS* (which arrived in NYC on May 15, 1922) that she was joining her Aunt Helen McConney there. Looking back on this adventurous move to the States, and in deciding to join her Aunt Helen, it was likely that she had spoken to or corresponded with, and exchanged stories and information about New York with many people, including her brother Cleve, her Aunt Helen and others (and of course the Gill family with whom she travelled). They would very likely have encouraged her to move to the USA to make a better life for herself. After all, St. Vincent was a tiny community, and neither her family, even such a close-knit one, nor her hometown, could offer her a great future.

In government records, Stella described herself on different occasions as a Governess and a dressmaker, and she was also a hairdresser as Iris Blanche (Sister), her niece, related to her children, Iris Murray and Randy. Iris Blanche told her children that she often spent school vacations with Aunt Stella when Goucher College was closed for school holidays, as she could not get back to her home in Puerto Rico very conveniently. I was told that she worked for a wealthy Jewish family in NYC as their Governess and cared for their child (or maybe children) in that capacity. She also knew the craft of dressmaking as she grew up in a sewing family. All of these vocations would have made her relatively independent and self-sufficient, especially in a city that was huge, impersonal and demanding.

In May 1928, Stella took a trip back to St. Vincent to visit her parents. After a six-years absence, I imagine she would have enjoyed telling them of her stories and adventures, and possibly about meeting her husband-to-be, another Vincentian who lived in New York, Arthur Gill. While I certainly do not know if such stories were told, the time frame lends itself to the probability.

Stella became a naturalized U.S. citizen in 1929 and she married Arthur Norman Gill (1891-1951), on April 19th, 1930. She was 28 and he was 38 when they were married. Uncle Arthur was a Building Superintendent for one or two high-rise buildings there. They remained in New York for many years. I recall being told by my mother that for many years, Aunt Stella sent back merchandise for her sisters to sell at *The Central Store* in Kingstown. As a boy, I did see some large packages arrive from her by mail, but don't know what they contained. She also sent Christmas gifts every year for Mac, Jen and myself, which we loved getting, as they contained exciting items (like toys, toy guns and dolls) that were not imported or available in the island, and likely would have been too pricy for our parents to readily purchase.

Aunt Stella was a strong family person, and, along with her husband Arthur, raised their only daughter, Mildred Ann. To check off her educational aspirations, she ensured Mildred went on to, and graduated from, secretarial school. They moved down to Tampa from New York, where unfortunately, Arthur passed away in 1951 when Mildred was only eight. Stella subsequently moved in with Mildred Ann and Ray (her husband), and their family, and lived with them in Fernandina Beach, Florida.

Aunt Stella came out from Florida to visit her sisters in Barbados while they and my parents, Ada and Alick, lived there – in the late 1970s. (I was living there also by then.) She always kept close to her sisters, and my mother always made a point of keeping up a steady correspondence with her. I drove my parents, Ada and Alick, to visit her and her family in Fernandina Beach in the early 1980s and she appeared to be doing well and enjoying her grands.

On a lighter note, I was told by Carol, her granddaughter, that Aunt Stella also loved M&M peanuts and the sunny beaches of Florida. She loved to accompany them to the beach and always ensured they did not have too much sun, as they might get badly sunburned.

Aunt Stella was a hard, loving and thoughtful worker. She passed away on Dec. 9th, 1984 at the age of 86.

*Reader's Notes*_____

_____

_____

_____

_____

_____

CHAPTER 13

MARY OLIVE LOUISE (MAISIE) McCONNIE

(1901-1965)

Mary Olive Louise, known by all her family and friends as Maisie, was the seventh child and fifth girl in the Richard Alleyne and Mary Elizabeth Anne McConnie family. She lived for six or seven years at Ratho Mill before moving to their new abode, *Clover Mead,* on Murray Road in Kingstown. She grew up more as a city girl in that respect, and her playmates would likely have been her many cousins who had moved down to town also.

I knew Aunt Maisie in my youth, so my information relating to her growing up is much like that of my knowledge of her siblings. I don't know if she was able to attend the Girls High School after its inception in 1911, as I have no knowledge of that. The age that schools of that day were accepting for its entrants was from 10 to 14 years of age, so she may have attended a government school. In 1911, the school fees were recorded as 6 pounds (£) per year (calculated at $178 at today's current rate of exchange). In any event, she was literate and according to my mother's records, started to work at Richards Bros. in Kingstown in 1919 (at the age of 18). My mother did not list any job type, but it was probably the ubiquitous term of 'clerk' which meant starting on one of the lower rungs of the work ladder.

After working in Kingstown for four years, she elected to leave for America on June 3rd, 1923 at the age of 22. She sailed to Barbados to catch the ship, the *S.S. VANDYCK*, that sailed for New York, arriving on June 12th, 1923 according to the ship's manifest. She reported on the ship's manifest that she was going to stay with her sister, Stella McConnie, and on a penciled-in note, it states that she was granted permanent admission to reside in the USA.[8]

Aunt Maisie stayed on and was married to Uncle Lisle – Carlisle McKerith Gill – (1898-1970) on Oct. 2nd 1926, in New York. They returned to St. Vincent at a future date (unknown), and had their first son, Gordon in May 1928. They had four children in total, Gordon (b.1928), Janice (b.1932), Brenton (b.1934) and Kendall (b.1937) who did not survive. They settled in St. Vincent and in later years, when I knew them in the 1950s and 1960s, they lived at Calliaqua on a beach property.

Uncle Lisle was financially successful as a local trader and had a partnership in the 'dry goods' store that became United Traders, Ltd. Aunt Maisie never worked after returning to St. Vincent to my knowledge. The couple loved the beach and boats and enjoyed the pleasures of sailing. They purchased a house (or perhaps built it) on a bay near to Calliaqua. It was the house in which I knew them as a boy. Uncle Lisle built a yacht which was called *WINSOME*, and they enjoyed sailing down the Grenadines with family and friends.

Aunt Maisie became a homemaker in St. Vincent, and Uncle Lisle and herself sent their two youngest children, Janice and Brenton to boarding school in Barbados and Brenton went on to McGill University in Canada to become a Mechanical Engineer. Janice became an executive with TWA. Their eldest son, Gordon, had a banking career with Barclay's Bank.

---

8. It is noteworthy that Aunt Maisie used a house name address for her father's residence as *Clover Mead*, Kingstown, St. Vincent on the ship's manifest. That may have been the name of the McConnie family house on Murray's Rd. in Kingstown. It was customary in those days for houses to be known by a name as part of their address.

Gordon married Betty Williams and they had two children, Deborah and Don. Janice married Graham Hayward, a chemical engineer, and they had two boys, Gavin and Peter. Brenton married Marlene Walker (a Trinidadian who had Vincentian connections) and they had two children, Kara and Robert.

Aunt Maisie, like all the McConnies, was a focused individual keen on family life and liked everything to be orderly. She kept in close contact with Ada and her sisters and enjoyed her family.

I do recall spending the occasional weekend with Aunt Maisie and Uncle Lisle, and spent lots of time discussing the plans he drew up for his next boat (which was never built). I particularly enjoyed climbing and eating the fruit of the plumrose tree in their backyard. (This fruit has different names in different islands, and was a small sweet pear-shaped fruit with a red edible skin and a snow-white interior with a luscious texture.)

They moved to Barbados shortly before Aunt Maisie passed away in 1965 and were buried there.

*Reader's Notes*_____

_____

_____

_____

_____

_____

CHAPTER 14

ERNEST NORBERT McCONNIE

(1903-1904) - (died as an infant)

Ernest Norbert McConnie was the third boy and eighth child of Richard Alleyne and Mary Elizabeth Anne McConnie. There is practically no information on him, the only info I have is that my mother (Ada) told me he died as an infant within a year of his birth (1903). She gave me the date of his birth, but the date of his passing I found in the St. Vincent archives as Feb. 9th, 1904. Ada, the youngest sibling, was born two years after he died, but recorded in her notes that her mother told her that he died of Croup. Ernest Norbert was born and also died at Ratho Mill.

*Reader's Notes*_____

_____

_____

_____

_____

CHAPTER 15

ADA ELAINE McCONNIE
(1906-1990) - (married W.A.G. "Alick" Nanton)

Ada Elaine was the ninth and last child born into the Richard Alleyne and Mary Elizabeth Anne McConnie family. Her birth certificate confirms that she was born at Ratho Mill. Like all children born late into a family, (her mother was 42 when she was born), she was likely spoiled by her older siblings and her parents but grew up with a sunny and inquiring disposition. She loved to laugh and was taught to cook, sew and play the piano.

Ada was able to go to the St. Vincent Girls High School for secondary school education, and she loved and excelled at several subjects including Mathematics and French (which she spoke with her version of a French accent). She joined the Girl Guides and became a stalwart proponent for guiding in St. Vincent for the rest of her life, becoming an Asst. Commissioner of the Trefoil Guild in her later years.

She left school with her school-leaving certificate. These certificates were given after passing an exam referred to as the Junior Cambridge – a precursor to the "O" & "A" Level Exam system that followed – and these exams were all adjudicated out of England. She then went to work for the GPO (General Post Office). She worked as a clerk for a Scotsman she called "Mr. Mac", who, she claimed, "worked their fingers to the bone." She mentioned that when a boat came to the harbour with mail for the island, it had to be sorted that same day. So, she worked many late hours into the night but said she enjoyed the camaraderie and friendship of her co-workers before she made her two-mile trek walking home.

On her religious side, she taught Sunday School at the Anglican Cathedral as did most of her sisters for several years. They never missed Sunday service and she took her kids to church religiously, whether it was for a 5am service or the Good Friday 3-hour marathon (12 noon to 3pm).

Of passing interest, all lower level pews in the Anglican Cathedral were reserved by a monthly subscription and carried a small frame with the congregants names that was updated continuously and jealously guarded. These were the days when you were not allowed to sit in the 'Smith' or 'Jones' pews even if they were empty. The upstairs gallery was taken up by pews for the less financially able without need for a reserved seating system.

Ada told us that she enjoyed her early days tremendously, and was popular with friends and boyfriends, none of whom she became serious with until she was in her 30s. From her own account, she was also the first female in St. Vincent to own and drive her own car. (For those days, this suggests she was an early Vincentian 'Women's Libber'.) Living at home and working for the government service, she was able to help with family expenses and enjoyed a decent standard of living.

Ada went to the USA in 1931 to a New York Girl Guide Jamboree. She regaled us with stories of the wonderful sites she saw and especially of the Coney Island rides and treats that must have made it the Disney World of those days. After the Jamboree, she stayed on for sometime with her sister, Aunt Stella, but I do not have more details of this visit. Her brother, Cleve, offered to send her to law school in the USA to further her career in life, but she told me that she was too settled, a bit scared of moving, and would not be close to her own family, so she never took up that generous offer from her brother.

Ada married Alick (W. Alexander G. Nanton) in 1940 at the age of 34. They moved to his family's estate at Biabou (primary crop grown was arrowroot), out in the country, where they had three children, MacGregor (1942), Jennifer (1943), and Geoffrey (1947). She essentially became a country wife for these years, but persuaded Alick to move back to Kingstown in 1950, where both his and her families resided. They moved in to *Granby Cottage*, next door to the Nanton family residence, *Granby Lodge*, where they remained until Alick purchased a house (*Melville*) on Murray's Road in 1956.

Ada hosted many meetings for charitable and service organizations – including the Thompson Home (for old ladies without financial means of support), the Trefoil Guild (Girl Guides of yesteryear), and the Old Girls Association (they provided support and scholarships to member's children who went on to the Girls High School and Boys Grammar School) groups. She was a friendly, jovial individual who developed a deep ongoing friendship with her best friend, May Munro, and enjoyed multiple friendships through her charitable and Girl Guide work with the wives of Parke and Parmie Eustace, the Wilsons (Katy and her sister), Mrs. Norris, Clarrie Paynter and many more of the ladies who were movers and shakers' in the Kingstown community. She never forgot her roots and enjoyed personal interaction.

Ada was remorseless with her children in their schoolwork, and would leave no stone unturned to ensure they learned and were educated to the max. She sent them to extraordinary teachers for extra lessons. The author was sent to Mr. Timmy Richards (a headmaster and bright mathematician with a Stentorian voice), Mr. Huggins and Mr. Crick (my BGS Headmaster who also had a great mathematical mind) among others, to ensure we mastered our schoolwork. These teachers afforded me a fast start in my overseas education and prepared us for life in general.

Ada's husband Alick purchased a plantation (Goldsborough Estate) along with his brother, Steinson, in the neighboring island of Tobago around 1956/57. This estate grew cocoa and coconuts.

However, Ada refused to go to Tobago to live as she considered it a backward island with inadequate schools (and she had no family there). So Alick then commuted between St. Vincent and Tobago. He would come home to St. Vincent by schooner every three or four months for a week or two to take care of his family as well as his family's business affairs there.

As soon as they could, Ada and Alick arranged to send their first two children for advanced schooling in England. Before leaving, they both passed their Junior School Certificate ('O' Levels later on). Mac studied Civil Engineering and Jennifer graduated in Catering. (After later moving to Canada in 1968, Mac concluded his education with a B.Eng. at Queens.) The financial hardship of keeping two children overseas (in the UK) at school was draining for them in the early 1960s, and Ada started to making jellies and jams to sell locally. This allowed her to ensure her youngest, Geoffrey, maintained his academic standing and she was able to continue serving on charitable and community boards like the old ladies Thompson Home, the Senior Girl Guides movement known as the Trefoil Guild in which she rose to Asst. Island Commissioner, as well as the "Old Girls Association" from the government Girls High School that promoted education for girls and boys on the island. She was a solid, dependable and industrious worker in these organizations.

Ada loved a good meal and missed a salad or two along the way. She had an incorrigible sweet tooth and made desserts frequently. She had a good sense of humor and enjoyed a good laugh (she loved jokes including those that were 'close to the bone' or could be classified as unfit for telling around a dining table). She loved life, her family and those around her.

Alick's plantation in Tobago was flattened by Hurricane Flora in 1963, and Dad, (Alick), tried to patch it back together; however, to bring the coconut and cocoa trees back into production, he would have had to replant and nurture them to maturity, and this would have taken from 5 to 7 years. So, in 1965/66, Alick and his brother, Steinson, sold the estate in Tobago. As he was getting older, Ada encouraged him to return to live in St. Vincent. He rejoined Ada, and shortly after they made the decision to move to Barbados, where there were established family connections. These included McConnie and Gill relations, and they decided to retire there. To complete the transition, they sent Geoffrey to Canada in 1966 to complete his studies at McGill, from which he graduated (B.Comm.) in 1970.

Alick and Ada then moved to Barbados with Ada's two sisters, Betha and Cecily, in 1967. They also moved to obtain better medical assistance. Betha and Cecily passed away in 1970 and 1972 respectively and Ada and Alick remained in Barbados until 1980.

So, as previously mentioned, Ada and Alick had three children:
- (A) MacGregor Richard Alexander married Marion Joy and they live in Canada. They had three children:
  - i. Paul married Junko and they have two children, Alex and Julia. They live in Japan.
  - ii. Ross married Christina (Chrissy) and they have two children, Nicholas (Nick) and Olivia and they live in Austin, TX.
  - iii. Meggan married Darren Sutherland (now deceased) and had one child, Jackson. They live in Edmonton, Alberta.
- (B) Jennifer Elizabeth married Guerdon (Jerry) Sauter, and they live in Florida, They had two children:
  - i. Deborah married Bryant Mendelson (now deceased) and they had no children. Deb lives in California.
  - ii Alison (unmarried) lives and works in Austin, TX.
- (C) Geoffrey Bernard married Helen Bowen and they live in Florida. They had two children:
  - i. Andrew (Andy) married Krista and they have two children, Oliver and Celeste. They live in Oregon.

    ii. Nicholas (Nick) married Kristina and they have three children, Brock, Bowen and Addison (Addie), and they live in Florida.

In spite of ageing issues, Ada enjoyed living in Florida with Alick, where two of her children (Jennifer and Geoffrey) and five grandchildren were living. Their son Mac and his family lived in British Columbia and they were able to visit them periodically. Ada was predeceased by Alick in 1988 and passed away at 83 in 1990.

*Reader's Notes*_____

_____

_____

_____

_____

_____

CHAPTER 16

SAMUEL BOXILL McCONNIE'S SECOND FAMILY

Samuel Boxill McConnie and Georgina/Georgiana (Lyder) Phillips had between five and seven children together but never got married. These children were baptised with the surname Lyder, but were subsequently given the McConnie name. Here are the names with a brief backstory taken from Ted McConnie's 'Family Forest' – it is not a current list, and probably dates back to the 1970s. I am unsure if the first two children, Edward Thomas and Frederick Bowen McConnie were Samuel's children. Some archival evidence implies that they were the children of his brother, another Edward Thomas McConnie.

1. **Edward Thomas McConnie (1855-?) – married Mary Elizabeth Cozier**
2. **Frederick Bowen McConnie (1861-1936) – married Sarah Williams**
3. **Aletha Blanche (Lyder) McConnie (1874-1953) – married Robert Carlton Layne (1867-1940)**
4. **Martha Lucretia (Lyder) McConnie (1857-??) – never married**
5. **Marianna Janette (Lyder) McConnie (1860-??)**
6. **Joseph Isaiah McConnie (1867 - ??)**

1. **Edward Thomas McConnie (1855-?) was the eldest son of this couple, and he married Mary Elizabeth Cozier in April, 1880.**
   They had two children:
   (A) Ella Alberta McConnie (1881-?), who was married three times. The first was to a Marshall, the second was to Frederick G. Wolfe, and third was to Robert H. Downing.
   (B) The second child was Ethel, who married a Banfield and had seven children:
      i. Olive Banfield, who married twice (the first was to Clement J Spring; no info on the second husband).
      ii. Muriel Banfield, who married Ottley Gill (no issue).
      iii. Ettie Banfield, who married Eddie McLeod and they had two children:
         a. Cynthia McLeod
         b. Thelma McLeod
      iv. Ira Banfield married a Vincentian, Galbraith Cropper, and they lived in St. Vincent. They had three children:
         a. Monty Cropper
         b. Renee Cropper
         c. Madeline Cropper
      v. Miriam married Bob Kennedy and they had one son, James.
      vi. Eitel (Bannie) Banfield, married his cousin, Leila Layne. They lived in St. Vincent and had three children:
         a. Annette, who married Bill Agard and lives in Trinidad.
         b. Leon, who married Josephine Sardine and they lived in St. Vincent.

  c. Marilyn, who married Richard
   Webster and lived in Trinidad.
 vii. Effie Banfield had one daughter:
  a. Patricia or Pat who married Noel
   Agard.

2. **Frederick Bowen McConnie (1861-1936)**
Frederick was Samuel and Georgina's second
son and was born in Barbados. He married Sarah
Williams (1866-1948) in 1887. They lived in St.
Vincent and had three children:
 (A) Bertram McConnie got married and
  reportedly lived in the U.S.A. from the
  1920's. He and his wife had two children.
 (B) Edna McConnie, who was married and
  died in 1953.
 (C) Thomas Lloyd McConnie. He married
  Evelyn Bradshaw from Dorsetshire Hill, St.
  Vincent and they had twelve children:
  i. Sarah Evelyn McConnie – married
   Vincentian Alexander Grant and they
   had three children:
   a. Diana Grant – born in
    St. Vincent.
   b. Joan Alexander Grant – born in
    Dominica.
   c. Margaret Grant – born in
    Barbados.
  ii. Clarice McConnie (b. 1927) – married
   Barbadian Herbert Webster and they
   lived in Barbados. They had two
   children:
   a. John Webster
   b. Alison Webster
  iii. Thomas Lloyd McConnie (b.1928)
   – married twice. His first wife was
   Marja Teryn, a Dutch Canadian, and

they had one child. His second wife was a Canadian, Susan Shepperd, and they had two children. His three children were:

    a. Suzanna McConnie – married Steven Atkinson and had three children:
- Steven, Jill and Liza

    b. Bowen Kendrick McConnie, a talented track & field athlete.

    c. Graeme Howard McConnie

iv. June Patricia McConnie (b.1930) – married a Vincentian, Othneil Leach, and they lived in Virginia, U.S.A. and had two children:

    a. Linda Leach who was born in Canada (married an American, Charles Alley and they lived in Washington, D.C.)

    b. Laura Lee Leach (also born in Canada).

v. Alison McConnie (b. 1932) – married a Barbadian, Rudolph Kirton, and they live in Vancouver, BC. They had two children:

    a. Wayne Kirton

    b. Roy Kirton

vi. Vera McConnie (b. 1935) – married a Barbadian, DeVere Cole, and they lived in Barbados. They had two children:

    a. Jennifer-Ann Cole (b. 1955) married an Englishman, Martin Beck, and they lived in Barbados. They had two children:
- Georgina (b.1978) and Joanna

b. Stephen Cole (b. 1957) married Deidre, an American and they lived in Philadelphia, PA. They had two children:
- Jared and Ashley

vii. Agnes McConnie (b. 1937) – married David Nicholls, a Barbadian involved in the construction business in Barbados. They had two children:

   a. Cheryl Nicholls who married a Barbadian, Steve Howard, and they had two children:
- Julie and Alan

   b. Elizabeth Nicholls

viii. Frederick Noel McConnie (b. 1938) – married a Barbadian, Janet Goddard. They lived in Barbados and had three children:

   a. Gregory

   b. Linda
   c. Ann Marie } twins

ix. Audrey McConnie (b. 1941) – married a Barbadian, Theodore Corbin and they moved to Australia. They had two children:

   a. Debra Corbin

   b. Sandra Corbin

x. Keith McConnie (b. 1943) – married Elizabeth Watson (a Barbadian). They live in Port Hope, Ontario, Canada and have three children:

   a. Jason

   b. Julie

   c. Sarah

(Our family grew up knowing Keith who was four years older than I was, and I knew him from Grammar School.)

    xi. Marcia McConnie (b. 1945) – married a Barbadian, Harold Fenty, and they lived in Barbados. No knowledge if they had any children.

    xii. Larry McConnie (b. 1947) – married an Englishwoman, and they live in Australia. They have three children:
      a. Mark
      b. Brett
      c. Kim
    (Author knew Larry and we attended the Boys Grammar School together.)

3. Aletha Blanche McConnie (1874–1953)
was the eldest daughter of Samuel and Georgina. In 1893, she married Robert Carleton Layne (1867-1940) and they lived in St. Vincent. They had fifteen children:

(A) George Carleton Layne (1895-1976) married three times and had two children:
    i. Carl Layne
    ii. Robert Layne

(B) Mabel Louise Layne (Aunt Lou) (1896-1975) who married Sydney Isaacs and they had two children. They lived in Trinidad and Tobago.
    i. Kenneth Isaacs
    ii. Lorna Isaacs

(C) Claude Harold Layne (1897-1971) (Uncle Claude) married a Grenadian, Osberga (Aunt Ossie) Banfield, and they lived in St. Vincent. They had three children:
    i. Desmond Layne m. Alice Preim and they had three children: Kim, Derek and Mark
    ii. Richard (Dick) Layne m. Valrae Davis and they had two children: Desmond and Carrie

iii. Erica Layne, who married Bernard (Barney) Abbott and they moved to Australia. They had three children.

(D) Ivy Carmen Layne (1898-1992), unmarried, was born in St. Vincent. She lived in NY for most of her life and moved to Florida at the age of 75. She had no children.

(E) Blanche Aletha Layne (1899-1985) married Leonard Gibson and they had two children:
   i. Allan Lester Gibson
   ii. Lenore Blanche Gibson

(F) Dorothy (Dolly) Amanda Layne (1901-1991) moved in the 1920s to the U.S.A. and married Henry Miller. They had one child:
   i. Sylvia Dorothy Miller married Jim Koford. (They had one child, James Koford) James had three children.

(G) Clifford S. Layne (1903-1966) married Doris Wilson. They had one child:
   i. Connie

(H) Leila Layne (1903-1955) married her cousin, Eitel (Bannie) Banfield and lived in St. Vincent. They had three children:
   i. Annette, who married Bill Agard and lives in Trinidad.
   ii. Leon, who married Josephine Sardine and they lived in St. Vincent.
   iii. Marilyn, who married Richard Webster and lives in Trinidad.

(I) Edwin Darwin Layne (1906-1991) – married Clara Nanton. They lived in St. Vincent and had three children:
   i. Errol Edwin Carlton m. Lenore Sardine. They had two children:
      a. Vanessa, who married Dustin Delany and had one child, Riley.
      b. Alex, who is unmarried.

ii. Deanna m. Bill Sadleir (They had two children: Alistair and Karen). She had a second marriage to Robert Hadley (no children).

iii. Winston – never married.

(J) Verton Randolph Layne (1907-1984) got married and went to live in Santo Domingo. They had four daughters:

i. Betty Layne

ii. Rita Layne

iii. Daisy Layne

iv. Maritza Layne

(K) Donald Ellery Layne (1909-1920) – died as a child at eleven from malaria.

(L) Frederick Evelyn Layne (1911-1979) married a Grenadian, Cynthia Glean. They lived in Barbados and had five children:

i. Aiden, married Ruth Maxwell and had two boys, Andrew and Christopher. They lived in Jamaica then eventually settled in Florida.

ii. Margaret Ann married an Englishman and they live in England.

iii. Paul (died in a traffic accident as a young man in Barbados).

iv. Mary Clare married a Barbadian 'Peacock' Rouett and they live in Vancouver, BC.

v. Patti married and lives in Vancouver, BC.

(M) Daisy Layne (1912-1990) married a dentist from St. Vincent, Louis Sprott, and had two children:

i. Elliott married Joy, a Vincentian and had two children.

ii. Terrance married Sonja Nanton, (the

author's first cousin), and they have three children:
 a. Kim who married a Connell from St. Vincent and lives there.
 b. Ryan who married a Vincentian and they have two daughters.
 c. Samantha who lives in Vancouver, BC.

(N) Ormyntrude Estalita Layne (1915-1917) – died as a child at two.

(O) Agnes Raymond 'Ray' Layne (1916-1983). She married Leslie Lord and they lived in Canada. They had one daughter: Beverly.

4. **Martha Lucretia McConnie (1857-??)** (who was known as Aunt Mattie) never married.

5. **Marianna Janette (Jane) McConnie (1860-??)** - She never married.

6. **Joseph Isaiah McConnie (1867-??)**
Joseph was born at Bawden's Land, St.Andrew in Barbados. He married Iva Gabriel about 1895 and they had two children:
 i. Clifford Edward Bowen McConnie
 ii. Winifred Elizabeth McConnie

CHAPTER 17

THE REST OF THE STORY

In a nutshell, St. Vincent is a beautiful place, a tropical haven, which will continue to be further developed as a tourist center, but its ability to sustain a burgeoning population is limited.

The settling of the McConnies in St. Vincent in the last quarter of the nineteenth century (ca.1875) and their departure or death by 1975 of most of their descendants, is the story of a family that made a risky move to escape a difficult and unpredictable life in Barbados. They moved to St. Vincent hoping to find an opportunity to survive and thrive. Today, very few of the family members remain there, but the reader can look at this account and readily understand why so many left in the twentieth century, for 'greener pastures' in Europe and North America.

The information discussed here does not carry a complete account of "the slings and arrows of outrageous fortune" that the McConnie family may have encountered, but it merely attempts to show the lifestyle of a family that aspired to a better life by moving to St. Vincent at that point in time. While this record compresses the lives and lifestyles mainly surrounding the Richard Alleyne McConnie family, this story attempts to give a history and lifestyle of the McConnie "Hundred-Year Affair" in order to acquaint future generations of McConnies and their offshoots, as well as other related families who have left St. Vincent over the years, with their "Vincentian roots."

It should be mentioned here that this genealogy is not without omissions. Records do not always identify parents of offspring that were born as a result of one-night-stands, secret trysts, drunken revelry or any other event. In official birth records, some mothers names are frequently mentioned in connection with a birth registration without any mention of a father. Throughout history, some fathers have been willing to acknowledge paternity and others have not. This pattern is not new, as we know, because children were born throughout the ages without any evidence of a father's name, and occasionally grew up without a mother's as well.

In concluding this history and genealogy, for the sake of completeness it should be mentioned that there would likely have been unrecorded McConnie stillborns and infant deaths at birth or shortly thereafter, a sad factor in everyday life of that era.

As you may have noted, this account is anchored in the 1950s and 1960s from the author's perspective. It is notably far from a comprehensive history, but attempts to reflect the experience of his own family as reflected at that point in time. The island has since moved on past many other milestones, so for an update, you will need to pursue that separately. The need for further related research is evident, but the author will leave this to future writers and generations to take up that challenge.

In closing, the author would like to leave you with a quote from his father-in-law, Harold Bowen, taken from his insightful repertoire:

"If every baby, like hallmark silver,
was stamped with it's maker's mark on the bottom,
what a revealing world it would be!"

APPENDIX A

Effects of British Colonization and the Colonial Development of Infrastructure on St. Vincent.

The effect of the British ownership on colonial St. Vincent was significant, and possibly even greater in the period of the McConnie saga as they put down their former Barbadian roots. As we have learned from history, using conquered territory to support and elevate any major nation is the cornerstone of colonization. This was certainly true for all world powers – including Spain, the Netherlands and Portugal – in the 17th to 19th centuries. World history also reminds us of this pattern that was well-established in the past—such as the Egyptian, Phoenician, Roman, Chinese and Viking dynasties of bygone days, to name a few. History also plainly shows that, in spite of our claims to be civil to each other, 'might trumps right' – even up to today.

While military and economic supremacy have always been the prime reasons for colonialization and colonization, the colonial pattern also requires that the victor – in this case Great Britain – elevate its subjugated nations to be as self-supporting as possible, and to contribute goods and services to the mother country. Two other goals in the conquer-and-rule playbook for the British Empire during the mid-18th to early 19th centuries were:

1. To support the steamships of the day by providing coaling stations for steam ships (e.g., Halifax, Jamaica and Bombay).
2. For military advantage (e.g., Gibraltar – which lasted into the twentieth century).

While this history is not a part of the McConnie saga, it is offered mainly to illustrate the effects of colonialization on St. Vincent. In the case of the smaller, underdeveloped colonies like St. Vincent, it was a monumental task to make it productive at that time. While this island may have had some basic military significance, it likely would have had more usage as a revictualling station for ships in the McConnie era as well as being a pawn in the chess game of the major world powers at that time.

It is notable that St. Vincent was used as a chess piece in the Treaty 'games' of the 18th century – being ceded to Britain in the Treaty of Paris in 1763. It was then seized and taken over by France in 1779. In the game of "winner-takes-all" St. Vincent was again restored to England in the Treaty of Gibraltar of 1783.

French influence in St. Vincent ended at this point, but the prior French domination of the island left a plethora of French names behind (e.g., La Soufriere, Grand Bonhomme, Petit Bordel, Chateaubelair, Grand Sable, Sans Souci and Mayreau, among many others), but no residual French language.

The colonialization of St. Vincent (as on the other British West Indian islands) shows a pattern of total British control. Britain used their governmental systems, financial support, administrative regulations and laws, including the establishment of record-keeping and controlled agricultural and educational systems, to accomplish their ends. Much of the administration was sorely needed to run the island, but the English leeched the Vincentian economy (as it did all colonies) to provide the Mother Country with agricultural products including sugar, cotton, tobacco and cocoa.

Employment and Occupations

In all likelihood, with the exception of the elite (British expats, plantation owners and businessmen), most residents would have worked very hard physically, in order to survive in that era and to make ends meet financially. Many with small plots would have grown their own fruits and ground provisions and would probably raised livestock and chickens to both sell/barter and feed themselves. Barter was common in those days, as it was a practical means for obtaining food or services without having much access to scarce cash.

Having laid the table of general occupation above, in Kingstown and some of the larger towns (such as Georgetown and Barrouallie), there would have been a number of Government (civil service) jobs. This would vary from porters to various department clerks and middle management – likely taken by the more educated in the community – typically English expatriates.

In poor town communities, with no reliable means of support, populated areas provided scanty means to survive outside of occasional daily employment. However, those living in rural areas could rely on the land to at least allow them to grow food to survive, but clothing was a genuine issue.

Education

In researching Government documents in St. Vincent, we learn that the St. Vincent Agricultural School (1900 thru 1914), was subsequently succeeded by the Boys Grammar School (1908 up to the present), The schools educated their pupils from the ages of 8 or 9 on up. This likely included schooling from elementary education up to secondary level. What we now regard as a kindergarten education, was probably taught at home if parents were up to the task. This would mean that many families were unable to pass along much of their education to their own children, and some likely never had any at all.

As I was growing up, the school system was based on the British model. From my own experiences, I know that in the 1950s and 60s, this included Government Elementary Schools for children ages 5 to 12, and Boys Grammar Schools and Girls High Schools both of which catered to the youth — ages 12 to 19. For the record, the elementary schools catered to both boys and girls, whereas the secondary schools in St. Vincent, as their names above denote, were not co-educational, and catered exclusively to boys or girls up to the age of 15 or 16. Beyond that point in the secondary schools, both sexes were often educated together – likely due to a scarcity of teachers as well as funds – in order to provide the higher level of learning that was required for University entrance. (This is not a forum to present an argument on boys and girls schools vs mixed/coed schools, but just wished to relay the school format that existed in St. Vincent and the British Commonwealth educational systems at that time.)

Transportation

From well before the 1800s and up to the mid-1900s, aside from walking everywhere, donkeys and donkey carts were an economical form of transport that were unregulated by the island's governing body. However, donkeys were well known as loud, stubborn and ornery. The new-fangled alternative that showed up in St. Vincent in the late 1800s or early 1900s was the use of bicycles. There were many variants (including the penny-farthing and the tricycle) before a bike with two equal-sized wheels, a pedal and a chain drive was developed to revolutionize simple, basic people transport.

At first, the bicycle was a phenomenon and a toy of the wealthy. With mass production, this machine soon became a competent and reliable means of transport – showing up in the first world war to carry people and information as needed. It spread to the colonies quickly and soon became the workhorse of messengers around the world. First owned by the affluent, both government and businesses in St. Vincent found them invaluable. English brands like "Humber" and "Raleigh" brought mechanical transport within the purchasing power of Vincentians. These were followed by the motorcycle in the 1930s and 1940s that pushed the speed of communication significantly.

Motorized transportation arrived in St. Vincent in the early 1900s. I am guessing that was sometime between 1910 and 1920.

I imagine that only a select handful of wealthy residents (perhaps ex-patriates, professionals or planters) could have owned motor vehicles. Up to this point, I believe that horse drawn carriages and conveyances would still have been in use. A major difficulty for public transport would have been the road system. Without some form of reliable footing, roads may have been unusable during heavy rains. I am guessing that broken rock and stone, because of their abundance on this volcanic island, may have been used to pave the more heavily travelled routes. Asphalt/ Tarmac would probably not have come into limited use in St. Vincent until the 1930s/1940s.

As St. Vincent wended its way into the twentieth century, four amphibious aircraft were first landed in Kingstown in 1927. This beginning was followed by the use of an airstrip at Diamond in 1932, (now the site of Argyle International Airport) which accommodated small planes and was the start of regular airmail and very limited passenger air travel. By the 1940s, the Diamond Airport was decommissioned due to the requirement for more up-to date air service. Following into the early 1950s, air mail and travel was instituted using the ubiquitous Grumman Goose (G21), an amphibious plane owned by British Guiana Airways that was of WWII vintage. This plane landed in the sea at Villa Airport dock and ramp. This was followed by the development of the Arnos Vale airport. This airport, which was renamed the E.T. Joshua Airport, had a main traffic highway that crossed the runway and was commissioned in 1962. (Fact: When there was a plane taking off or landing, the road was barred using long bamboo poles to prevent any traffic from crossing the runway at the same time as a landing plane.) This was the history of air passenger travel up to the end of the era under discussion.

Nutrition/Food

Nutrition is always a product of availability and cost. St. Vincent had a ready supply of fish, ground provisions and fruit, much of which were homegrown, cheap and plentiful. Livestock meats available locally were limited and not very cheap in comparison.

Imports were more expensive, and the wholesalers in Kingstown made money by importing cheap supplements— (Irish) potatoes, rice from overseas, especially Guyana, and salted codfish from Newfoundland. Consequently, feeding most of the population was accomplished by using local agricultural products, fish and livestock, along with imported foodstuffs if you could afford it.

Fish was a good source of protein and was readily caught off the coasts. Fishermen plied these coasts daily and caught dolphin (mahi-mahi), kingfish and redfish, among many others. Fish were caught by both seine (nets) and by hook and brought in fresh every day. Shellfish, including lobsters and conch, were popular. Tri-tri (frey or tiny fish) were caught at the river mouths with fine nets/muslin cloth and harvested and made into fishcakes. Imported salted codfish from Newfoundland (known locally as saltfish), was a cheap, supplementary source of protein.

The St. Vincent international allocation for whales were limited to one or two catches per year for large whales, but the meat was blubbery and odorific. There were and are larger catches of smaller whale species that are not tracked. Current catch limits from the IWC is four whales per year. Despite the strong gamey flavor and odor, whale meat was relatively cheap and not wasted.

Ground provisions were a source of carbohydrates and vitamins which were easily grown in the fertile wet soil. The starchy vegetables probably represented most of the caloric intake of the island's residents in the period under review. The island grew almost all of what it consumed in vegetables, not counting imported potatoes and rice. Being a lush tropical island, ground provisions including sweet potatoes, yams, dashenes, eddoes and cassava were plentiful and cheap, often grown by homeowners themselves.

In addition, the abundance of the breadfruit was a lifesaver to most of the population. As is well documented, Captain Bligh brought the breadfruit from the South Seas island of Tahiti to St.

Vincent in 1793. The breadfruit tree *(Artocarpus altilis)* grows to a height of about 85 feet (26 m). The rough-skinned fruits are about the size of very large grapefruits – ball-shaped with a typical diameter of 9-10 inches. This was brought to the West Indies by Captain Bligh and was originally meant to feed slaves. However, over the years, it has become a national dish, enjoyed by all. One of the popular meals was roasted breadfruit and 'bulchow' (a saltfish and succulent vegetable mix).

The availability of fruit in St. Vincent is especially good. One of the most popular, mangoes, were brought from India and other tropical venues initially. The island soon developed a reputation for excellent fruit (as did the other Windward Islands of Grenada, St. Lucia and Dominica). As a boy, I enjoyed the many varieties of mangoes, along with plums, guavas, bananas, limes, papayas, custard apples and soursop, along with lesser-known fruits like shaddock, plumrose, Java plums, tamarinds, sapodillas, etc.

Growing up, many of the succulent fruits appeared to grow wild. Those fruit growing near a private land boundary were often considered 'for the taking' – much to the chagrin of the owners. In addition, there were many other fruits, nuts, corn and vegetables grown there, but often in smaller quantities and sold locally. As St. Vincent has such rich volcanic soil and can grow most anything, there are probably many other edible agricultural products that were grown that I have not mentioned.

Animals raised domestically for meat included chickens, sheep, goats, pigs, and cows. So, while there was some availability of chicken, lamb, goat, pork and beef, they tended to be expensive. (I recall the local beef was particularly tough.) As you can imagine, theft of livestock was common in a poor community, and tracing the origin of meat after the animal was slaughtered is obviously impossible.

The Vincentian population also harvested small quantities of land crabs, lobsters, turtle meat, birds and crayfish, along with any other sources of protein that they could find. Consequently, feeding most of the population was accomplished by using local agricultural products, local fish and livestock, along with any imported foodstuffs one could afford.

Health

The Vincentian population tended to care for its own health in the absence of enough medical doctors. While many in the younger Vincentian population seemed reasonably healthy during the period in question, there were many issues with medical help availability that told the sad tale of inadequate health care.

I do recall that in the period under review, malnutrition and infant mortality were major problems. Growing up in the 1950s and 1960s, I was also aware of many tropical fevers and respiratory diseases typical in a tropical environment. Diseases were often introduced by visitors and visiting sailors and spread rapidly in the humid climate. Fevers were ever present, as were a host of tropical diseases (e.g., malaria). Added to that was the combination of available cheap rum and poor nutrition that provided other harmful issues to the health of many in the community.

I have not lived there in the subsequent period (from 1966 to the present), so I cannot make any objective health commentary on the general health of Vincentian population for this later period, but maintaining good health was always an issue for Vincentians. As in all underdeveloped countries, self-medication was prevalent throughout the population, and often the only available solution. There were a variety of native bush teas, natural laxatives (e.g., senna leaves boiled into a foul-tasting liquid) and other home remedies used to obtain better health.

As mentioned earlier, there was still the use of leeches to bleed off the 'bad blood' that caused certain diseases and illnesses. My brother was the recipient of one of those sessions. In the homemade category, I was given a variety of awful-tasting bush teas and native laxatives to rid my body of whatever I was supposed to have.

I could add, however, that I was aware that improved health programs were ramped up by each successive Vincentian government to combat diseases and malnutrition – often with the help of the WHO and UNICEF. A personal example was my vaccination in the 1950s for polio at the government-run elementary school I attended (Kingstown Preparatory School). I also recall doctors from all around the world being recruited to attend to our various maladies, emergencies and wellbeing. And even then, they were in short supply. Medical attendance was sometimes available for emergencies at hospitals, and all doctors made house calls if they were available.

All in all, health was generally ok for younger, healthy Vincentians, but as individuals aged, the difficulty of obtaining medical specialists, medication, medical tests and hospital care was a major challenge for this third world country.

Lighting – Sources of Lighting

Another difficulty of life in St. Vincent during the McConnie period was finding a satisfactory source of energy to provide light and heat for everyday life. The capital of Kingstown had oil lamp light poles in use from the 1920s. Before that, without personal candles, torches or oil lamps, candle or lamp light from inside buildings was all that was available to help one get around, unless it was a moonlight night.

In fact, many students in the 1800s into the first half of the 1900s studied by candle and lamp light according to my mother. This lamp light practice continued well into the 1960s (in the period the author lived in St. Vincent) because of brownouts and blackouts that lasted for hours and sometimes for days. As noted in the following section on communications and electricity, some rural areas were still not being served by an electrical supply up to when I left St. Vincent in 1966, as the country simply could not afford it.

Finding efficient and inexpensive sources of energy to provide light at night was a vital economic factor in the life of all Vincentians. The use of candles, torches and oil lamps in St. Vincent to provide light in the period under review was pervasive. Kerosene lamps and lanterns were frequently used at night and most dwellings had them. Kerosene was imported as were candles (made from a variety of animal and vegetable fats and oils). In St. Vincent, both oil lamps and candles were used until electrical light and power was available.

Well into the 1960s (when the author lived in St. Vincent), with a fairly dependable electrical supply, most households still depended on candles, torches and oil lamps in an emergency, because periodic brownouts and blackouts lasted from hours to days. As noted earlier, some rural areas were still not being served by an electrical supply up to when I left St. Vincent in 1966.

(Note: The tropical daylight hours in St. Vincent are typically between 6am to 6pm – with small variations – because St. Vincent lies close to the Equator.)

Communications

For communications, Vincentians would have had to rely on word-of-mouth, letters and messages to connect with each other. Locally, where word of mouth was inconvenient or impossible, messengers could deliver notes on foot or by bicycle. Pedestrian messengers were in common use by government, businesses, private individuals, and even for long distances.

There, even in those days, mail was sent throughout the islands by sea—surface mail. Air mail, started in 1927, and grew in fits and starts to a more regular service in the 1930s.

It was not until the 1930s that the government bought and installed a used wired-telephone system from the USA for St. Vincent. The telephone system I grew up with in the 1950s was of the old exchange-type vintage, where an attendant at the main exchange in Kingstown asked who you wished to contact and then they connected both parties with wired plugs. You remained on the line while they rang the phoneline of the party you wished to speak with. Of course, there were also the party lines that required one, two or three rings to alert and speak to the right party. (My home phone number in the 1960s, for example, was a mere two digits – our number was 97. (Side note: In the 1950s and 1960s, my family's P.O. Box number was 55 and there was no house delivery of mail.)

A telegram (cable) service was also established for the islands sometime in the first half of the twentieth century – in the 1920s or 1930s. I do not know a date for this, but telegrams (cables) were used in the 1940s to send critical information in a timely manner, and by the 1950s, no wedding was complete without cable wishes being read at the reception from family or friends overseas. The telegram service was made possible by a wire cable that physically connected St. Vincent, as part of a chain network with other neighboring islands, to England and the U.S.A.

Electricity

One of the advantages of having a mountainous topography and a rainy climate was that St. Vincent was able to develop and install a hydroelectric supply of power. This machinery was installed in the rivers there, sometime in the 1930s/40s and remains a consistent supply of electricity for a portion of the needs of the island up to now.

Around the same time as telephones were becoming available, St. Vincent imported and installed an electrical supply service in Kingstown. In 1931, the first electrical supply was made available to its first 32 customers. From that point on, distribution continued in the town, and after Kingstown was adequately supplied, more distant districts were hooked up as was economically viable. Again, because of the island's mountainous terrain, many districts in remote areas were among the last to be electrified. I recall many districts not getting electricity for decades because of cost and accessibility.

As I was growing up during the 1950s and 1960s, I recall the brownouts and blackouts that plagued the electrical system. With prevalent rainstorms, frequent lightning, and uneven terrain to deal with, these proved a daily challenge for the Electric Company to maintain consistent service. Added to those circumstances, there were periodic earthquakes to contend with from the active volcano, La Soufriere. In fact, I recall our house walls shaking, the ground underfoot vibrating and hanging pictures moving on the walls. It was a feeling of helplessness during the more intense earthquakes.

Summary

The above history and commentary on the Effects of British Colonialization and its Colonial Development on St. Vincent is a recap of the author's observations and research for the era in question. While the author was born into a relatively privileged family in 1947, his experiences did not render him oblivious or unsympathetic to many of the deprivations he noted.

Growing up in this cauldron, however, did allow him to marinate in and personally experience, the trials and tribulations as well as the developmental advances made, on the island. This section is therefore yet another reason to share a slice of his genealogically-slanted history of St. Vincent. He hopes his family and interested friends will reap some benefits from his efforts.

In spite of the difficult or unusual circumstances of the era under discussion, St. Vincent has been a nesting ground that has spread, and continues to spread positive, lasting and meaningful changes throughout the world.

APPENDIX B

McCONNIE RECIPES

Item #1

Recipe for RICE WINE – A sweet dessert wine

(Copied Mar. 11th 2022, from Ada (McConnie) Nanton's handwritten recipe.)

■ Recipe found dates back to the 1940s and was likely an old recipe.

Ingredients:

1. – 5 lbs. white sugar
2. – 6 bottles of water (Rum bottles - 26oz bottles)
3. – 8 large oranges
4. – 6 large limes
5. – 1 oz yeast
6. – 2 egg whites and egg shells
7. – ¾ lbs. raisins (crushed)
8. – ¾ lbs. prunes (crushed)
9. – 1 ¼ lbs. rice

Oranges and limes must be *peeled and squeezed*, using the juice only.

Wash rice well.

Add all ingredients (except yeast and eggs) with rice to water and stir well to get the sugar melted.

Lastly, *add* yeast and well-beaten whites of eggs and crushed egg shells.

Set for 14 days in large earthenware jar and cover with thin cloth for four (4) days. Then, cover tightly.

Stir every day.

On 15th day, do not stir. *Strain* through muslim and let settle for three (3) days. (Tip: On 15th day when you strain, *pour off* clear liquid into another container to settle, and put thick residue into separate container to settle.)

You then bottle off and get rid of sediment by *decanting* into another bottle. Should be ready in three (3) months, but taste improves with age. This is a sweet wine.

My notes: Pls. note that I was an observer occasionally when the wine was being made, but I am pretty sure that the sugar used by my mother was of the clear granular West Indian type, a clear cane sugar, as opposed to a light brown sugar. (It was not the refined super-fine granulated sugar or caster sugar used for sweetening teas or coffees.)

Item #2

Recipe for WAR-TIME CAKE

(Also copied from a handwritten recipe sent to Ada. My disclaimer: No idea how it tastes as I have never tried it. This was sent to her about 1941 as far as I can tell.)

Ingredients:

1. – ¼ lb. table butter
2. – 1 lb. sugar
3. – 1 lb. flour
4. – 3 eggs – well beaten
5. – 2 tsp. baking powder
6. – ¼ lb. mixed fruit (raisins, currants, etc.)
7. – Vanilla essence
8. – 1 pt. milk or enough to make a soft cake mixture

Cut butter into flour and baking powder as for pastry. *Add* sugar and *mix* well. *Add* eggs *well-beaten* and mixed in with some of the milk and *add* floured fruit and more milk as necessary. *Bake* in a 9-inch pan.

This can be chocolate iced or if you leave out the fruit, cut in half and put chocolate icing between the halves, or any other trimmings you fancy.

Author's notes: When looking at the ingredients above, bearing in mind I can't cook even though I can boil water, I was surprised at first to see that eggs, butter and flour were ingredients included during WWII when all imports were affected. I suspect that eggs were plentiful as chickens were kept by most small farmers and households. And then there was table butter and flour? I recall the butter made by my aunts churning the cream that settled on top of the milk they received. The raw milk was boiled to pasteurize it. As it cooled, the cream was ladled off the top and saved for making butter. They churned it by hand and added salt to make it edible. (Don't ask for details as I only observed the process.) I was told that during the war, flour in the Caribbean was made from local starchy vegetables, e.g., breadfruit, yams, cassava and arrowroot. Finally, most of the islands, being of volcanic origin and fertile, had good agricultural land, so home-grown foods and fruits were plentiful.

APPENDIX C

<u>The Island of Saint Vincent</u>

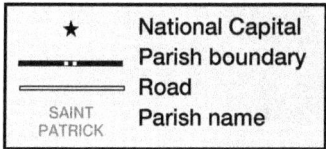

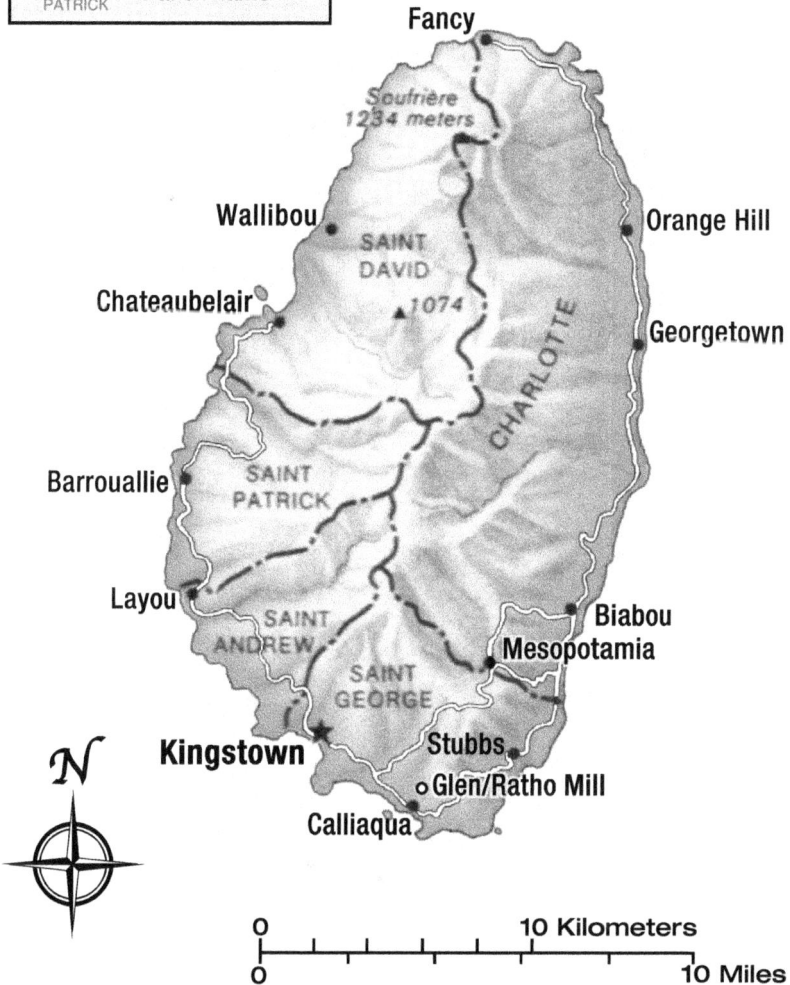

★	National Capital
▬	Parish boundary
═	Road
SAINT PATRICK	Parish name

Fancy

Soufrière
1234 meters

Wallibou

SAINT DAVID

Orange Hill

Chateaubelair

▲1074

Georgetown

CHARLOTTE

Barrouallie

SAINT PATRICK

Layou

SAINT ANDREW

Biabou

Mesopotamia

SAINT GEORGE

Kingstown

Stubbs

Glen/Ratho Mill

Calliaqua

N

0   10 Kilometers

0   10 Miles

Saint Vincent and the Grenadines

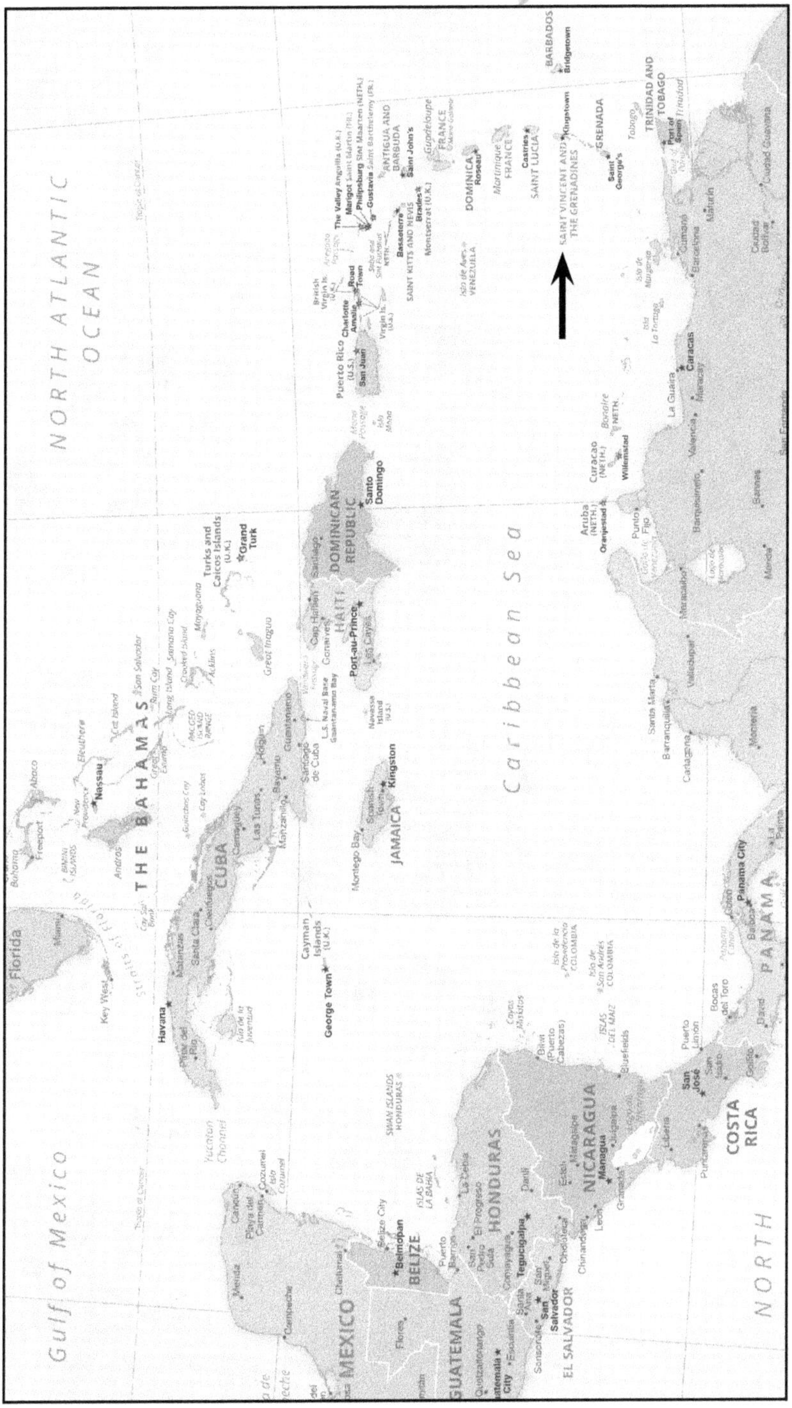
NORTH ATLANTIC OCEAN
Gulf of Mexico
Caribbean Sea
THE BAHAMAS
CUBA
Havana
Nassau
Florida
Key West
Turks and Caicos Islands (U.K.)
Grand Turk
HAITI
Port-au-Prince
DOMINICAN REPUBLIC
Santo Domingo
JAMAICA
Kingston
Cayman Islands (U.K.)
George Town
Puerto Rico (U.S.)
San Juan
ANTIGUA AND BARBUDA
Saint John's
SAINT KITTS AND NEVIS
Basseterre
DOMINICA
Roseau
SAINT LUCIA
Castries
SAINT VINCENT AND THE GRENADINES
Kingstown
GRENADA
Saint George's
BARBADOS
Bridgetown
TRINIDAD AND TOBAGO
Port of Spain
Aruba (NETH.)
Oranjestad
Curaçao (NETH.)
Willemstad
Caracas
MEXICO
BELIZE
Belmopan
GUATEMALA
HONDURAS
Tegucigalpa
EL SALVADOR
San Salvador
NICARAGUA
Managua
COSTA RICA
San José
PANAMA
Panama City
NORTH

REFERENCES & RESOURCES

1. *"The McConnie Family in Barbados"* E.M. (Ted) McConney:1966. This was APCG updated by his son, Gerry E. McConney: 1988 and by P.G. (Gerry) Bowen: 2000.

2. *The Redlegs of Barbados,* E.T.Price, article published in ACPG Yearbook, Vol.19. (1957) – pp.35-39.

3. *Making Whiteness, Remaking Empire: The Poor Whites of Dorsetshire Hill, St. Vincent 1834–1940,* Connor E.R, DeMerchant, PhD Student, Univ. of New Brunswick:

4. *"Walk und Nyam Buckras": Poor White Emigration from Barbados, 1834-1900,* Watson, Karl, 2000. Journal of Caribbean History 34:137-46.

5. *Experiments in Indenture: Barbados and the Segmentation of Migrant Labor in the Caribbean 1863-1865,* Lawrence Brown, Centre for Cross-Cultural Research, Australian National University.

6. *Archaeology Below the Cliff: Race, Class, and Redlegs in Barbadian Sugar Society,* Matthew C. Reilly.

7. *At the Margins of the Plantation: Alternative Modernities and an Archaeology of the "Poor Whites" of Barbados.* Matthew Connor Reilly, Syracuse University (8-2014).

8. Barbados Church Records, 1637 – 1887

9. The websites: Ancestry.com, FamilySearch.com, MyHeritage. com, Geni.Com.

10. Handwritten Dates, Events and Details of the family: Ada (McConnie) Nanton and from the meticulous research of our cousin - Connor DeMerchant.

www.ingramcontent.com/pod-product-compliance
Lightning Source LLC
Chambersburg PA
CBHW060503280326
41933CB00014B/2840